Better Homes and Gardens
SALAD BOOK

BETTER HOMES AND GARDENS BOOKS
NEW YORK • DES MOINES

CONTENTS

On the cover: Chunks of blue cheese top the succulent vegetables in Summer Salad Bowl.

Left: Plan for generous helpings when the main dish is Deviled Beef Toss.

This Low-calorie Symbol appearing throughout the Salad Book identifies accompaniment salads, main dish salads, and salad dressings that will fit well into a calorie-controlled menu. For a complete listing, see the Index.

Our seal assures you that every recipe in the *Salad Book* is endorsed by the Better Homes and Gardens Test Kitchen. Each recipe is tested till it rates high in family appeal, practicality, and deliciousness.

RAINBOW OF FRUIT SALADS

Fruits as colorful as the rainbow brighten any dinner table. Combinations can be chosen to add a splash of color to the meal and a sunny flavor to the menu. In this chapter, sketches and pictures showing arrangements of fresh and canned fruits help the food artist.

Fruit-studded salads can be planned for any colorful course in the menu. Side dish salads compliment a hot dish. Try them arranged, molded, frozen, or refrigerated. When a baked dish doesn't seem appealing, feature fruit as the main dish.

Fruit salads such as the multilayer gelatin salads add a dazzling note and flavor contrast to that buffet menu. Use the purchasing guide and quantity recipes to aid planning and preparation for the party.

Fruit and Orange Fluff is one of the easiest salads to prepare. Just whip up the dressing from an instant pudding mix, then serve with a luscious mixture of cut fresh fruit.

SIDE DISH SALADS

FRUIT AND ORANGE FLUFF

Try the salad shown on previous page—

1 3⅝- or 3¾-ounce package
   instant vanilla pudding mix
2 cups cold milk
1 cup dairy sour cream
½ teaspoon grated orange peel
¼ cup orange juice
   Sliced unpared pears*
   Quartered nectarines *or* peaches*
   Whole fresh strawberries
   Seedless green grape clusters
   Fresh dark sweet cherries
   Fresh blueberries

To prepare dressing, slowly beat pudding mix and milk in mixing bowl with rotary beater till well blended, about 1 to 2 minutes. Gently beat in sour cream. Fold in orange peel and juice. Chill.

To serve, center small bowl of dressing in large shallow bowl. Arrange fruits around. To keep cold, place fruit bowl atop bowl of crushed ice. Makes 3 cups dressing.

*To keep fruit bright, use ascorbic acid color keeper or dip in lemon juice mixed with a little water.

MELON SALAD

1 3-ounce package cream cheese,
   softened
2 tablespoons mayonnaise or
   salad dressing
2 tablespoons milk
¼ cup diced celery
2 tablespoons chopped pecans
½ cup frozen whipped dessert
   topping, thawed
3 cups chilled melon balls

With rotary beater, beat together first 3 ingredients till smooth and fluffy. Add celery and nuts; fold in thawed topping. Chill. Divide melon balls into 6 lettuce cups; top each serving with cheese mixture. Serves 6.

CHEESE-TOPPED PEARS

½ cup plain yogurt
¼ cup cream-style cottage cheese
2 tablespoons mayonnaise or
   salad dressing
1 tablespoon blue cheese
1 29-ounce can pear halves,
   drained and chilled

Blend together first 4 ingredients. To serve, spoon a little cheese mixture over center of each pear half. Makes ¾ cup dressing.

MELON SUPREME

1 13½-ounce can pineapple tidbits
1 cup small cantaloupe balls
1 cup small watermelon balls
1 cup sliced, peeled fresh
   peaches*

. . .

¼ cup mayonnaise or salad
   dressing
1 tablespoon confectioners' sugar
¼ teaspoon grated lemon peel
½ cup whipping cream, whipped

Drain pineapple, reserving 2 tablespoons syrup. Mix fruit together; chill. Blend together reserved syrup, mayonnaise, and sugar; beat with rotary beater till smooth. Stir in lemon peel. Fold chilled fruit into mayonnaise mixture. Fold in whipped cream. Chill. Makes 6 to 8 servings.

SWISS APPLE SALAD

Combine 4 medium unpared apples, diced*; 1 cup diced Swiss cheese; ½ cup diced celery; 1 cup dairy sour cream; and dash salt. Chill thoroughly. Serves 6 to 8.

CORING FRESH PEARS

For neat looking fresh pear halves, core them with a melon ball cutter or teaspoon.

PEAKED PINEAPPLE SALAD

2 cups melon balls
1 cup sliced pitted dates
2 medium bananas, peeled and
  sliced (2 cups)
1/4 cup chopped macadamia nuts *or*
  chopped toasted almonds
• • •
1 cup whipping cream
2 tablespoons sugar
1 tablespoon lemon juice
  Dash salt
1 20 1/2-ounce can pineapple slices,
  chilled (10 slices)

Combine melon balls, dates, bananas, and nuts. Whip cream with sugar, lemon juice, and salt till soft peaks form. Fold into fruit mixture. Top each lettuce-lined plate with one pineapple slice; pile fruit mixture over. Makes 10 servings.

FRESH FRUIT AND CREAM

Have all ingredients and salad bowls well chilled. Line individual salad bowls with a bed of coarsely shredded lettuce. For each serving, arrange rings of fresh pink grapefruit sections; fresh white grapefruit sections; fresh strawberries; watermelon cubes; figs with centers filled with seeded purple grape halves; and papaya slices.

Garnish with sprigs of watercress frosted with confectioners' sugar. Serve with Whipped Cream Dressing.

Whipped Cream Dressing: Combine 1 cup mayonnaise or salad dressing; 1/2 cup whipping cream, whipped; and 1 teaspoon honey. Tint with red food coloring to a delicate pink. Makes 1 1/2 cups dressing.

SHERRY SPICED PEARS

Drain one 29-ounce can pear halves, reserving 1/2 cup syrup. In saucepan, combine reserved syrup, 1 cup brown sugar, 1/2 cup dry sherry, 2 tablespoons vinegar, 1 tablespoon chopped candied ginger, and 1/4 teaspoon ground cinnamon. Stir mixture over medium heat till sugar is dissolved. Add drained pear halves and simmer 5 minutes. Serve pears hot or cold.

CINNAMON-APPLE SALAD

Prepare these crimson red salads in the fall when apples are at their best—

1/2 cup (4 ounces) red cinnamon
  candies
2 cups water
6 small tart apples, pared and
  cored
• • •
1 3-ounce package cream cheese,
  softened
2 tablespoons milk
1 teaspoon lemon juice
1/3 cup pitted dates, snipped
1 8 3/4-ounce can crushed pineapple, drained (3/4 cup)
2 tablespoons chopped walnuts

In a 3-quart saucepan, cook cinnamon candies in water till dissolved. Add apples and cook slowly, uncovered, just till tender, about 15 to 20 minutes, turning once during cooking. Refrigerate apples in syrup several hours, turning once.

Blend together cream cheese, milk, and lemon juice till smooth and creamy. Add dates, drained pineapple, and walnuts. Drain apples; stuff centers with cream cheese mixture. Serve on lettuce-lined plates. Serves 6.

ORANGE-PEAR SALAD

Toasted sesame seed decorates the top—

1 cup dairy sour cream
2 tablespoons honey
1/4 teaspoon grated orange peel
• • •
2 large oranges, peeled
6 pears, pared, halved, and cored
1 head Bibb lettuce
1 tablespoon toasted sesame seed

To make dressing, blend sour cream with honey and orange peel. Cut each orange into six slices. For each salad, spread one orange slice with sour cream-honey dressing; top with second orange slice.

Insert orange "sandwich" between two pear halves; place on lettuce-lined plates. Top with remaining dressing. Sprinkle with sesame seed. Makes 6 servings.

FRESH FRUIT BOWL

In large lettuce-lined salad bowl, arrange 6 small pared watermelon wedges as dividers. Between dividers, place separate mounds of peach slices*, bias-cut banana slices*, halved avocado rings*, cantaloupe and watermelon balls, orange sections, and halved pineapple rings.

Center salad with flaked coconut. Tuck in sprigs of mint for garnish. Serve with Blue Cheese Fluff Dressing.

*To keep banana, avocado, and fresh peach slices pretty and bright, use ascorbic-acid color keeper or dip pieces in lemon juice mixed with a little water.

Blue Cheese Fluff Dressing: Mash 2 ounces (½ cup) blue cheese with rotary beater; gradually beat in ⅓ cup salad oil till smooth. Beat in ½ cup dairy sour cream, 1 tablespoon lemon juice, and ½ teaspoon grated lemon peel. Add milk, if desired, to make fluffy consistency. Chill. Makes 1¼ cups dressing.

GREEN AND GOLD SALAD

1 medium papaya
1 cup salad oil
⅓ cup tarragon vinegar
¼ cup sugar
1 tablespoon lime juice
½ teaspoon *each* salt, dry mustard, and instant minced onion
¼ teaspoon paprika
4 cups mixed salad greens

To peel ripe papaya, dip in boiling water one minute, then place in ice water. With tip of paring knife, pull away peel. Cube papaya, reserving seeds.

To make dressing, place remaining ingredients *except* papaya and salad greens in blender container. Cover; blend thoroughly. Add 1½ tablespoons papaya seeds; blend till seeds are size of coarsely ground pepper. Chill. Combine papaya and greens. Toss with desired amount of dressing. Serves 6.

An arrangement of brilliant red anthuriums sets the mood for a festive Hawaiian Isle dinner. Exotically-dressed Green and Gold Salad creatively complements pork roast and baked bananas.

SLIM-TRIM FRUIT TOSS

- 2 medium oranges, pared and sliced
- 1 cup halved strawberries
- 1 cup cubed watermelon
- ½ cup plain yogurt
- ¼ cup low-calorie strawberry jelly
- 1 to 2 drops red food coloring

LOW CALORIE · LOW CALORIE ·

Combine first 3 ingredients; chill. Beat together yogurt and jelly; blend in food coloring. Serve fruit on lettuce-lined plates. Pass dressing. Makes 4 to 6 servings.

CREAMY AMBROSIA SALAD

- 2 medium oranges, pared and diced
- 2 medium bananas, peeled and sliced
- 1 cup halved seedless green grapes
- ½ cup pitted dates, snipped
- ¼ cup frozen whipped dessert topping, thawed
- ¼ cup mayonnaise or salad dressing
- ¼ cup flaked Toasted Coconut (see Index)

Drain diced oranges. Combine oranges with next 3 ingredients; chill. Fold dessert topping into mayonnaise; fold into fruits. Spoon into crisp lettuce cups; sprinkle with coconut. Makes 4 to 6 servings.

PINEAPPLE-CHEESE SALAD

- 1 20½-ounce can pineapple chunks
- 1 16-ounce carton (2 cups) cream-style cottage cheese
- 2 cups miniature marshmallows
- ½ cup pitted dates, snipped
- 1 tablespoon lemon juice
- 6 to 8 whole pitted dates

Drain pineapple, reserving ¼ cup syrup. Combine reserved syrup and next 4 ingredients. Mound cheese mixture on lettuce-lined plates; arrange pineapple chunks around. Top each serving with one whole pitted date. Makes 6 to 8 servings.

FIG FRUIT SALAD

- ½ cup dried figs
- 1 8¾-ounce can crushed pineapple
- 1 3-ounce package cream cheese, softened
- 1 tablespoon mayonnaise or salad dressing
- 1 tablespoon honey
- • • •
- 2 medium unpared apples, diced
- 2 medium bananas

Steam figs in a sieve over hot water about 20 minutes; cool. Clip stems; cut figs in thin strips. Drain pineapple, reserving 2 tablespoons syrup. Beat syrup, cheese, mayonnaise, and honey together till smooth. Toss figs, apples, and drained pineapple with dressing. Chill. Before serving, peel and slice bananas; toss with fruit mixture. Serves 6.

PEAR WALDORF SALAD

- 2½ cups diced unpared pears
- 1 tablespoon lemon juice
  Dash salt
- 1 cup diced celery
- ½ cup raisins
- ¼ cup coarsely chopped walnuts
- ¾ cup mayonnaise or salad dressing

Sprinkle pears with lemon juice and dash salt. Add celery, raisins, and nuts. Toss with mayonnaise; chill. Makes 6 to 8 servings.

PINEAPPLE STYLES TO KNOW

Crushed: Fruit is cut in very small pieces just right for molded salads and dressings.

Tidbits: Slices are cut into small wedges that are more dainty than chunks. Add to tossed salads and fruit cups.

Chunks: Even, spoon-size pieces cut from thick slices are available canned or frozen. Frozen chunks should *not* be used when preparing gelatin salads.

Spears: Lengthwise strips make good additions to salad plates and trays.

Slices: Rings are cut from the pineapple cylinders. They can be used in, under, or atop salad combinations.

LOW-CAL FRUIT BOWL

1 medium grapefruit, chilled
2 medium oranges, chilled
1 ripe medium banana
1 cup chilled sliced fresh
    strawberries
½ cup chilled honeydew balls
    Mint sprigs
    Low-cal Snow Dressing

Peel and section grapefruit and oranges, reserving juices. Peel and slice banana; brush with reserved fruit juices. Combine grapefruit and orange sections, banana, strawberries, and honeydew balls in lettuce-lined bowl. Trim with mint. Serve with Low-cal Snow Dressing. Makes 4 servings.

Low-cal Snow Dressing: Combine 1 cup plain yogurt, 1 teaspoon lemon juice, and dash salt. Stir in non-caloric liquid sweetener equal to 4 teaspoons sugar. Chill.

TROPICAL APPLE SALAD

1 cup diced unpared red apple
1 cup diced unpared yellow apple
1 large banana, peeled and sliced
1 cup sliced celery
½ cup broken walnuts
½ cup flaked coconut
¼ cup mayonnaise or salad
    dressing
1 tablespoon sugar
½ teaspoon lemon juice
    Dash salt
½ cup whipping cream, whipped
    Romaine leaves

Combine apple, banana, celery, walnuts, and coconut. To prepare dressing, blend together mayonnaise, sugar, lemon juice, and salt. Fold whipped cream into mayonnaise mixture; gently fold into apple mixture. Chill.

Arrange romaine in bowl; spoon in salad. Garnish with additional unpared apple slices, if desired. Makes 6 servings.

← **A profusion of red and yellow apples,** bananas, celery, nuts, and coconut in a creamy dressing tempts every hungry palate. Tropical Apple Salad measures up to all flavor expectations.

SPICED WALDORF SALAD

3 cups diced apple
2 teaspoons lemon juice
        • • •
1 cup diced, drained canned spiced
    apple rings (6 to 8 rings)
1 cup halved seedless green
    grapes
½ cup chopped celery
½ cup chopped walnuts
⅓ cup mayonnaise or salad
    dressing

Sprinkle fresh apple with lemon juice; add spiced apple, grapes, celery, and walnuts. Fold in mayonnaise. Chill. Serve on lettuce-lined plates. Makes 6 to 8 servings.

MIDDLE EAST PEARS

Sweet and sharp go together in a jiffy—

1 29-ounce can pear halves,
    chilled and drained
1 cup plain yogurt
¼ cup sugar
    Ground nutmeg *or* cinnamon

Place pear halves on lettuce-lined plates. Combine yogurt and sugar; spoon into pear cavities. Sprinkle with nutmeg.

PINEAPPLE CHEESE-WICHES

1 20½-ounce can pineapple slices,
    chilled
1 3-ounce package cream cheese,
    softened
2 tablespoons mixed chopped
    candied fruits and peels
    Curly endive

Drain pineapple slices, reserving 2 teaspoons syrup. Beat cream cheese with 1 to 2 teaspoons syrup till of spreading consistency. Stir in candied fruits and peels.

Blot pineapple slices with paper toweling. Spread cream cheese mixture on 5 pineapple slices; top each with another pineapple slice. Cut each "sandwich" in half. For each salad stand 2 halves on edge on curly endive-lined plate. Makes 5 servings.

Bright red strawberries add flavor and color to an unusual side-dish salad. The combination includes sliced peaches, crosswise slices of kiwi, and whole strawberries on crisp leaf lettuce.

Plump, juicy blueberries and fresh pineapple chunks fill the hollow and cascade down the side of a honeydew melon wedge. Serve this salad in a shallow bowl and pass a fluffy cooked dressing.

Bananas, cut in chunks on the bias, are arranged on lettuce leaves with pitted red plum halves and succulent red raspberries. To keep bananas bright, brush with a little lemon juice mixed with water.

FRUIT COMBINATION GUIDE

Team the fruit with suggested counterparts at the right for a real taste treat. Then, arrange items on different varieties of greens each time. Top with a dressing.

To Go Along With	Choose These
Unpared red apple slices	• Grapefruit sections, sliced avocado, and pomegranate seeds
Unpared red apple wedges	• Cream cheese balls rolled in finely chopped nuts
Apple, diced	• Mandarin orange sections and diced celery
Avocado, peeled and sliced	• Grapefruit sections and persimmon wedges • Sliced tomato
Apricots, halved and seeded	• Red grapes and sliced jellied cranberry sauce • Pineapple chunks and maraschino cherries
Banana, halved lengthwise	• Orange and grapefruit sections and pitted dates • Cottage cheese and salted peanuts
Banana, bias-cut	• Halved red plums, sliced pineapple, red raspberries, and coconut
Figs, halved and seeded	• Raspberries and cream cheese balls rolled in shredded coconut
Grapefruit sections	• Sweetened raw cranberries • Orange sections, pineapple spears, and ripe olives
Honeydew melon, pared and crescent-cut	• Thinly sliced Prosciutto ham
Honeydew melon, pared and sliced	• Raspberry, lemon, or lime sherbet
Melon, pared and sliced	• Fresh sweet cherries, halved green grapes, and chopped pecans • Fruit cocktail and whipped cream
Melon, cubed	• Cottage cheese and fresh strawberries • Raspberries and bias-cut banana slices
Peach, halved	• Blueberries and raspberries • Cottage cheese and candied ginger
Peach, spiced	• Pineapple chunks and apple-mint jelly
Pear, halved	• Shredded American cheese • Sliced plums and blueberries • Halved green grapes and cream cheese
Pineapple, chunks	• Orange sections and fresh strawberries
Pineapple, sliced	• Watermelon chunks and sliced banana

FRUIT ARRANGEMENTS

Combine fresh and canned fruits to create an enticing salad. Line plates with leaf lettuce. Place banana quarters, orange sections, and a peach half on each. Trim with berries.

For a frilly effect, line the plate with curly endive. Make a circle of grapefruit sections around outside edge. Fill center with unpared apple slices and melon balls. Garnish with nuts.

Romaine leaves also make an attractive salad liner. Place leaves in star fashion on each plate. Mound plum halves and cantaloupe balls inside each ring. Insert clusters of grapes and raspberries in any open area.

On each Bibb lettuce-lined plate, arrange banana quarters, crosswise slices of orange, dates, and a few blackberries. To transform the salad into an ideal side dish to serve in winter, substitute grapes for the blackberries.

Center cottage cheese on each lettuce-lined plate. Around it place a pear and peach half, each filled with berries; halved pineapple slices; strawberries; grapes; and mint.

This patriotic salad is red, white, and blue. Atop each leaf lettuce-lined plate place a large pear half. Fill the cavity with blueberries. Set spiced crab apple wedges around each pear half.

←**Chicken salad** hides beneath fresh fruits—orange sections; strawberries; avocado balls; halved limes; and unpared pineapple, sliced lengthwise—for a party-perfect summer main dish. Establish a tropical mood by lining each plate with a bamboo place mat and by garnishing the salad with pineapple leaves and fragrant gardenias. For added refreshment, serve with tall glasses of well-chilled tea.

FRUIT-FILLED MOLDS

BERRY-PEACH MARBLE

1 3-ounce package strawberry-
  flavored gelatin
2 cups sliced fresh strawberries
1 16-ounce can peach slices
1 envelope (1 tablespoon)
  unflavored gelatin
2 tablespoons lemon juice
1 2-ounce package dessert topping
  mix
2 3-ounce packages cream cheese,
  softened

Dissolve strawberry-flavored gelatin in 1 cup boiling water; stir in 1 cup cold water. Chill till partially set. Fold in berries.

Meanwhile, drain peaches, reserving syrup. Dice peaches. Add enough water to peach syrup to make 1 cup. In saucepan, soften unflavored gelatin in syrup mixture; heat and stir till gelatin is dissolved. Stir in lemon juice. Cool. Prepare dessert topping mix following package directions; beat in cream cheese. Fold in peach-gelatin mixture and diced peaches. Chill till partially set.

Layer strawberry and cheese gelatin mixtures in 7½-cup mold. Swirl knife through gently to marble. Chill till firm. Serves 10.

MELON POLKA-DOT MOLD

2 3-ounce packages cherry-
  flavored gelatin
1 tablespoon lemon juice
1 8-ounce package cream cheese
½ cup finely chopped pecans
2 cups small melon balls

Dissolve gelatin in 2 cups boiling water. Stir in 1¾ cups cold water and lemon juice. Pour 1 *cup* gelatin into 6½-cup ring mold. Chill till partially set. Shape cheese into 40 balls; roll in nuts. Arrange 9 *each* cheese and melon balls alternately in mold. Chill till *almost* firm. Meanwhile, chill remaining gelatin till partially set; fold in remaining cheese and melon balls. Pour over gelatin in mold. Chill till firm. Makes 8 to 10 servings.

PAPAYA RING MOLD

Dissolve two 3-ounce packages lemon-flavored gelatin in 2 cups boiling water. Stir in 1 cup cold water, one 8¾-ounce can undrained crushed pineapple, and 3 tablespoons lemon juice. Chill till partially set.

Fold into gelatin 1 large papaya, peeled, seeded, and diced (1½ cups), *or* one 15-ounce can papaya, drained and diced; 2 medium oranges, peeled, sectioned, and cut up; and two 3-ounce packages cream cheese, chilled and diced. Pour into 6½-cup ring mold; chill till firm. Makes 8 to 10 servings.

CHICKEN PECAN SALAD

3 medium peaches, peeled and
  sliced (1½ cups)
3 cups cubed cooked chicken
1 cup diced celery
½ cup mayonnaise
2 tablespoons salad oil
1 tablespoon vinegar
¼ cup toasted broken pecans
  Cranberry Ring

Reserve a few peach slices for garnish. Cut up remaining peaches. In large bowl, combine cut up peaches, chicken, and celery. Blend together next 3 ingredients and ½ teaspoon salt; toss with chicken mixture. Chill. Before serving, fold in nuts. Serve in center of Cranberry Ring. Garnish with peaches and parsley, if desired. Makes 6 servings.

Cranberry Ring: Dissolve two 3-ounce packages lemon-flavored gelatin and ¼ teaspoon salt in 1 cup *each* orange juice and water, heated to boiling. Stir in 1 cup cold orange juice. Chill till partially set. Stir in one 16-ounce can whole cranberry sauce. Pour into 6½-cup ring mold. Chill till firm.

Toasted pecans, fresh peaches, and hearty →
chunks of chicken fill the center of ruby Cranberry Ring. Adorn the Chicken Pecan Salad with choice peach slices and fluffs of fresh parsley.

FRUITY GINGER ALE MOLD

A red and gold bubbling beauty—

1 3-ounce package lemon-flavored
    gelatin
1 cup boiling water
1 7-ounce bottle (about 1 cup)
    ginger ale, chilled

   . . .

1 unpared apple, cut in wedges
½ cup chopped pared apple
½ cup halved seedless green
    grapes
1 8¾-ounce can pineapple tidbits,
    drained (⅔ cup)

Dissolve gelatin and dash salt in boiling water. Cool to room temperature. Slowly add ginger ale. Chill till partially set.

Arrange apple wedges in 5½-cup mold. Pour in a little gelatin mixture. Chill till *almost* firm. Add pared apple, grapes, and pineapple tidbits to remaining mixture. Pour over first layer. Chill till firm. Serves 5 or 6.

Cran-cheese Squares are artfully placed on a marble plate and trimmed with orange sections.

HONEY BANANA MOLD

1 6-ounce can evaporated milk
1 3-ounce package orange-flavored
    gelatin
2 ripe medium bananas
¼ cup honey
3 tablespoons lemon juice

Pour milk into freezer tray. Freeze till soft ice crystals form around edges. Dissolve gelatin in 1 cup boiling water; cool. Peel bananas; mash in large mixer bowl with electric mixer. Beat in honey and lemon juice, then cooled gelatin. Chill till mixture is partially set.

Whip mixture at low speed while gradually adding icy cold milk. Increase to high speed; continue whipping till double in volume and thick. Pour into 4½-cup mold. Chill till firm. Makes 4 to 6 servings.

CRAN-CHEESE SQUARES

1 3-ounce package orange-
    pineapple-flavored gelatin
1 cup orange juice
½ cup whipping cream, whipped
1 3-ounce package cream cheese,
    softened
¼ cup chopped pecans

   . . .

1 envelope (1 tablespoon)
    unflavored gelatin
1 16-ounce can whole cranberry
    sauce
2 tablespoons lemon juice
¼ teaspoon ground allspice
⅛ teaspoon ground nutmeg
1 cup orange sections
1 7-ounce bottle (about 1 cup)
    ginger ale, chilled

Dissolve orange-pineapple-flavored gelatin in 1 cup boiling water; stir in orange juice. Chill till partially set. Blend a little whipped cream into cheese; fold in remaining cream. Add nuts; fold into partially set gelatin. Pour into 9x9x2-inch pan; chill till *almost* firm.

Soften unflavored gelatin in ¼ cup cold water; stir over low heat till gelatin is dissolved. Combine next 5 ingredients; stir in gelatin. Gradually stir in ginger ale. Pour slowly over cheese layer. Chill till firm. To serve, cut into squares. Makes 9 servings.

FRUIT-NUT CHEESE MOLD

1 20½-ounce can (2½ cups)
   crushed pineapple
1 3-ounce package lime-flavored
   gelatin
2 3-ounce packages cream cheese,
   cubed and softened
1 cup diced celery
½ cup chopped walnuts
¼ cup chopped canned pimiento
1 cup whipping cream, whipped

Heat undrained pineapple to boiling. Add gelatin; stir till dissolved. Slowly add hot mixture to cheese, beating smooth with rotary beater. Chill till partially set. Stir in celery, nuts, and pimiento. Fold in whipped cream. Pour into 6½-cup mold. Chill till firm. Makes 6 to 8 servings.

SPARKLING MELON LOAF

2 envelopes (2 tablespoons)
   unflavored gelatin
1 6-ounce can frozen lemonade
   concentrate, thawed
2 7-ounce bottles (about 2 cups)
   ginger ale, chilled
2 tablespoons maraschino cherry
   juice
2 cups frozen honeydew balls,
   thawed and drained, *or* 2 cups
   fresh honeydew balls
2 tablespoons sliced maraschino
   cherries
¼ cup dairy sour cream
¼ cup mayonnaise or salad
   dressing

Soften gelatin in ½ cup cold water; stir over low heat till gelatin is dissolved. Add ¾ cup cold water and lemonade concentrate. Slowly add ginger ale. Divide gelatin mixture in half. Stir cherry juice into first half; chill till partially set. Fold melon balls and cherries into partially set gelatin. Pour into 8½x4½x 2½-inch loaf dish. Chill till *almost* firm.

Meanwhile, add sour cream and mayonnaise to second half of gelatin mixture. Beat with rotary beater till smooth. Leave at room temperature till fruit layer in mold is *almost* firm. Then slowly pour sour cream mixture over. Chill till firm. Makes 8 to 10 servings.

ORANGE-PINEAPPLE RING

Molded sunshine to tempt the palate—

2 envelopes (2 tablespoons)
   unflavored gelatin
½ cup sugar
¼ teaspoon salt
2 cups orange juice
   • • •
2 3-ounce packages cream cheese,
   cubed and softened
1 cup cold orange juice
1 13½-ounce can (1⅔ cups)
   crushed pineapple

In saucepan, combine gelatin, sugar, and salt; stir in 2 cups orange juice. Stir over medium heat till gelatin is dissolved. Gradually beat hot gelatin mixture into cream cheese; add 1 cup cold orange juice and undrained crushed pineapple.

Chill till partially set, stirring occasionally. Pour into 6½-cup ring mold; chill till firm. Makes 8 to 10 servings.

Made with frozen or fresh honeydew, this Sparkling Melon Loaf is an appetite tempter.

APPLE-CHEESE RIBBONS

1 16-ounce can (2 cups)
   applesauce
1 3-ounce package lime-flavored
   gelatin
2 tablespoons lemon juice

. . .

1 envelope (1 tablespoon)
   unflavored gelatin
1 12-ounce carton cream-style
   cottage cheese, sieved
1 3-ounce package cream cheese,
   softened
¼ cup mayonnaise or salad
   dressing
½ cup diced celery

Heat applesauce and ⅔ cup water to boiling. Add lime-flavored gelatin and lemon juice; stir till gelatin is dissolved. Cool. Reserving *half* of mixture, pour remainder into 8½x 4½x2½-inch loaf dish. Chill till *almost* firm.

In saucepan, soften unflavored gelatin in ½ cup cold water. Stir over low heat till gelatin is dissolved. Blend cheeses and mayonnaise; stir in gelatin and celery. Mix well. Pour into dish over first layer. Chill till *almost* firm. Pour reserved applesauce mixture over cheese layer. Chill till firm. Serves 8.

GOLDEN APRICOT MOLDS

Spiced with cinnamon and cloves—

1 30-ounce can apricot halves
2 tablespoons vinegar
7 whole cloves
4 inches stick cinnamon
1 3-ounce package orange-
   flavored gelatin
1 8-ounce can jellied cranberry
   sauce, cut in 8 slices

Drain apricots, reserving syrup. Add next 3 ingredients to reserved syrup; bring to boiling. Simmer, uncovered, 10 minutes. Strain syrup and measure; add enough boiling water to make 2 cups. Pour over gelatin; stir till gelatin is dissolved. Chill till partially set.

Arrange drained apricot halves in eight ½-cup molds and pour gelatin mixture over. Chill till firm. To serve, unmold on cranberry slices. Makes 8 servings.

ORANGE-GRAPEFRUIT RING

2 3-ounce packages orange-
   flavored gelatin
1 6-ounce can frozen orange
   juice concentrate, thawed
1 11-ounce can mandarin oranges
1 16-ounce can grapefruit
   sections, drained and cut up

Dissolve gelatin in 1½ cups boiling water; add juice concentrate and 1 cup cold water. Drain oranges, reserving syrup. Add syrup to gelatin mixture. Chill till partially set. Fold in oranges and grapefruit. Pour into 6½-cup ring mold. Chill gelatin mixture till firm. Makes 8 to 10 servings.

CRANBERRY MOLD

Relish mold for Thanksgiving dinner—

Dissolve one 3-ounce package *each* cherry-flavored and lemon-flavored gelatin and ½ cup sugar in 3 cups boiling water. Add 1 tablespoon lemon juice and one 8¾-ounce can undrained crushed pineapple; chill till gelatin mixture is partially set.

Fold in 2 cups whole fresh cranberries, ground; 1 small unpared orange, quartered, seeded, and ground (about ⅔ cup); 1 cup diced celery; and ½ cup chopped walnuts. Pour gelatin mixture into 8½-cup mold. Chill till firm. Drain one 20½-ounce can pineapple slices. Serve salad with pineapple slices. Makes 10 to 12 servings.

FRUIT COCKTAIL MOLD

1 17-ounce can fruit cocktail
1 3-ounce package lime-flavored
   gelatin
1 7-ounce bottle (about 1 cup)
   ginger ale, chilled
2 tablespoons lemon juice

Drain fruit cocktail, reserving syrup. Add enough water to syrup to make 1 cup; heat to boiling. Add gelatin and stir till dissolved; cool. Gently stir in ginger ale and lemon juice. Chill till partially set. Fold in drained fruit. Pour into 3½-cup mold. Chill till firm. Makes 4 or 5 servings.

FRUIT-NECTAR SALAD

Dissolve one 3-ounce package lemon-flavored gelatin in one 12-ounce can (1½ cups) apricot nectar, heated to boiling. Add ½ cup cold water and 1 tablespoon lemon juice. Chill till partially set.

Fold in one 11-ounce can mandarin oranges, drained; ½ cup diced unpared apple; and ½ cup halved seedless green grapes. Pour gelatin mixture into 4½-cup mold. Chill till firm. Makes 4 or 5 servings.

FRUITED EMERALD WREATH

A pineapple-studded gem—

> 2 3-ounce packages lime-flavored gelatin
> 1 20½-ounce can pineapple slices
> 2 tablespoons lemon juice
> 1½ cups seedless green grapes

Dissolve gelatin in 2 cups boiling water. Drain pineapple, reserving syrup. Add lemon juice to reserved syrup and enough cold water to make 2 cups. Add syrup mixture to gelatin; chill till partially set. Fold in grapes.

Pour gelatin mixture into 6½-cup ring mold. Place pineapple slices on edge, 2 together, at 5 intervals around mold. Chill till firm. If pineapple extends above gelatin, trim off ends before unmolding so mold will sit flat. Makes 10 to 12 servings.

JELLIED AMBROSIA

A gelatin variation of a Southern favorite. Serve with mayonnaise or whipped cream—

In saucepan, mix 1 envelope (1 tablespoon) unflavored gelatin and ¼ cup sugar together; add ½ cup cold water. Stir over low heat till gelatin and sugar are dissolved. Add 1¼ cups orange juice and 1 tablespoon lemon juice. Chill till partially set.

Segment 2 medium oranges, peeled; cut segments in pieces, reserving a few whole segments for garnish. Fold orange pieces; 1 medium banana, peeled and sliced; and ¼ cup flaked coconut into gelatin. Pour into 4½-cup mold. Chill till firm. Unmold; trim with reserved orange segments. Serves 6.

SHRIMP IN AVOCADO RING

Lemon wedges, to serve with the shrimp, make an appropriate garnish—

> 1 3-ounce package lemon-flavored gelatin
> 1 cup mayonnaise or salad dressing
> 1 to 2 tablespoons lemon juice
> ½ teaspoon salt
> 2 medium avocados, peeled and sieved (1 cup)
> 1 cup whipping cream, whipped
> Lettuce
> Cleaned and cooked shrimp

Dissolve gelatin in 1 cup boiling water. Chill till partially set; whip till fluffy. Stir in mayonnaise, lemon juice, and salt. Fold in avocado and whipped cream. Pour into 5½-cup ring mold or six to eight ½-cup ring molds. Chill till firm.

Unmold on lettuce; fill center with shrimp. Makes 6 to 8 servings.

BLUE CHEESE FRUIT CUPS

> 1 16-ounce can fruit cocktail
> 2 envelopes (2 tablespoons) unflavored gelatin
> 2 cups orange juice
> 1 3-ounce package cream cheese, cubed and softened
> ½ cup mayonnaise or salad dressing
> ¼ cup lemon juice
> 2 tablespoons sugar
> 1 ounce blue cheese, crumbled (¼ cup)
> ½ cup broken pecans

Drain fruit cocktail, reserving 1 cup syrup. Soften gelatin in *half* the reserved syrup. Heat orange juice just to boiling and add to softened gelatin, stirring till gelatin dissolves. Slowly add hot mixture to cream cheese, beating with rotary beater till smooth.

Add remaining reserved fruit syrup, mayonnaise, lemon juice, sugar, and dash salt. Beat gelatin mixture again till smooth. Chill till partially set. Stir in drained fruit cocktail, blue cheese, and nuts. Spoon into ten ½-cup molds. Chill till firm. Serves 10.

PLUM DESSERT SALAD

2 envelopes (2 tablespoons)
    unflavored gelatin
1 cup sugar
2 cups orange juice
¼ cup lemon juice
2 cups fresh red plums, pitted
    and cut in wedges, *or* 1
    16-ounce can plums, well-
    drained and pitted
Lemon Sauce

Combine gelatin and sugar; add 1½ cups cold water. Stir over low heat till gelatin and sugar are dissolved. Add orange and lemon juices. Chill till partially set. Set pan of gelatin in ice water; beat with rotary beater till light and foamy. Fold in plums. Pour into 6½-cup mold; chill till firm. Unmold; top with wreath of flaked coconut, if desired. Pass Lemon Sauce. Makes 8 servings.

Lemon Sauce: Beat 2 eggs and 1 tablespoon lemon juice together till thick and lemon-colored. Gradually add 1 cup sifted confectioners' sugar, beating constantly. Stir in ½ teaspoon vanilla, ¼ teaspoon grated lemon peel, and dash salt. Makes 1¾ cups.

ORANGE DELIGHT SALAD

Drain one 11-ounce can mandarin oranges, reserving syrup; add enough water to reserved syrup to make ¾ cup. Dissolve two 3-ounce packages orange-flavored gelatin in 2 cups boiling water. To *half* the gelatin add reserved syrup-water mixture; chill till partially set. Fold in oranges and ¼ cup broken pecans. Pour into one 6½-cup mold or ten to twelve ½-cup molds. Chill till gelatin mixture is *almost* firm.

Meanwhile, spoon 1 pint vanilla ice cream into remaining hot gelatin; stir till ice cream is melted. Chill till mixture mounds when spooned. Fold in 1 medium banana, peeled and sliced. Spoon over orange layer; chill till firm. Makes 10 to 12 servings.

Plum Dessert Salad will star at a luncheon or late evening get-together. Crown the mold with a delicate ring of moist coconut and be certain that fluffy Lemon Sauce accompanies each serving.

APPLE RING WALDORF

    1 3-ounce package lemon-flavored
        gelatin
    1 medium unpared apple
    2 teaspoons lemon juice
    2 tablespoons chopped walnuts
    ½ cup miniature marshmallows
    ⅓ cup chopped celery
    ½ cup mayonnaise or salad
        dressing

Prepare gelatin following package directions; chill till partially set. Pour a little gelatin into 6½-cup ring mold. Cut enough thin apple wedges to fit bottom of mold; lay wedges with unpared side out, around outside edge of mold. Chill till *almost* firm.

Dice remaining apple; sprinkle with lemon juice and fold into remaining gelatin. Fold in nuts, marshmallows, celery, and mayonnaise. Spoon on top of first layer. Chill till firm. Makes 6 servings.

FROSTED FRUIT MOLD

    1 3-ounce package lime-flavored
        gelatin
    1 7-ounce bottle lemon-lime
        carbonated beverage, chilled
    1 8¾-ounce can crushed pineapple
    1 medium banana, peeled and
        sliced
    ¼ cup sugar
    1 tablespoon all-purpose flour
    1 slightly beaten egg
    ½ cup whipping cream, whipped
    ¼ cup shredded sharp process
        American cheese
    2 tablespoons grated Parmesan
        cheese

Dissolve gelatin in 1 cup boiling water; cool. Slowly add carbonated beverage. Chill till partially set. Drain pineapple, reserving syrup. Fold drained pineapple and banana into gelatin mixture. Pour into 8x8x2-inch pan. Chill till firm.

Combine sugar and flour in saucepan and stir in reserved syrup and egg. Cook and stir over low heat till thickened; chill. Fold whipped cream into egg mixture. Spread over gelatin. Sprinkle with cheeses. To serve, cut into squares. Makes 6 to 8 servings.

MOLDED CHERRY RING

    1 20-ounce can pitted tart red
        cherries (water pack)
    2 envelopes (2 tablespoons)
        unflavored gelatin
      Non-caloric liquid sweetener to
        equal ¾ cup sugar
    5 drops red food coloring
            • • •
    ½ cup lemon juice
    ¼ cup chopped celery

Drain cherries, reserving juice; add enough water to juice to make 3 cups. Soften gelatin in juice mixture; stir over medium heat till gelatin is dissolved. Add sweetener, food coloring, and cherries; bring just to boiling.

Remove from heat; add lemon juice. Chill till partially set, stirring occasionally. Fold in celery. Pour into 5½-cup ring mold. Chill till firm. Makes 8 or 9 servings.

CITRUS-CHEESE SQUARES

    2 16-ounce cans grapefruit
        sections
    2 3-ounce packages lemon-flavored
        gelatin
            • • •
    1 8-ounce package cream cheese,
        softened
    2 tablespoons milk
    ⅓ cup chopped walnuts
            • • •
    ¼ cup halved maraschino cherries

Drain grapefruit, reserving syrup; add enough water to syrup to make 3½ cups. Heat *half* the syrup mixture to boiling, then add to gelatin and stir till dissolved. Add remaining syrup mixture; cool.

Arrange *half* the grapefruit sections in bottom of 9x9x2-inch pan. Carefully pour *half* the gelatin mixture over arranged fruit; chill till firm. Blend cream cheese with milk and chopped walnuts. Spread cheese mixture over firm gelatin layer; chill.

Meanwhile, chill remaining gelatin mixture till partially set. Arrange remaining grapefruit and cherries on top of cheese layer. Carefully pour partially set gelatin mixture over fruit. Chill till firm. To serve, cut into squares. Makes 9 to 12 servings.

SEA LIME SALAD

Dissolve one 3-ounce package lime-flavored gelatin in 1 cup boiling water. Gradually stir hot gelatin into one 8-ounce package cream cheese, cubed and softened; beat till smooth. Chill till partially set.

Fold in one 8¾-ounce can undrained crushed pineapple; 1 cup chopped pared cucumber; ¼ cup chopped walnuts; and ½ cup whipping cream, whipped. Pour into 5½-cup mold; chill till firm. Serves 5 or 6.

PEACH-A-BERRY SQUARES

 2 3-ounce packages orange-flavored gelatin
 3 medium peaches, peeled and sliced
 1 cup fresh or frozen blueberries
 ¼ cup dairy sour cream
 ¼ cup mayonnaise or salad dressing

Dissolve gelatin in 2 cups boiling water; stir in 1½ cups cold water. Chill till partially set. Fold in peaches and blueberries. Pour into 8x8x2-inch pan; chill till firm. Blend together sour cream and mayonnaise; spread mixture over firm gelatin. To serve, cut into squares. Makes 9 servings.

GOOSEBERRY CUPS

The piquant flavor enhances a turkey dinner—

 1 16-ounce can gooseberries
 2 3-ounce packages lemon-flavored gelatin
 ½ cup sugar
 2 cups orange juice
 1 cup sliced celery
 ¼ cup broken walnuts

Drain gooseberries, reserving syrup. Add enough water to syrup to make 1½ cups; add gelatin and sugar. Heat to boiling, stirring till gelatin and sugar are dissolved. Remove from heat. Stir in orange juice. Chill till partially set. Fold in drained gooseberries, celery, and nuts. Pour into ten ½-cup molds. Chill till firm. To serve, unmold on lettuce-lined plates. Makes 10 servings.

QUICK SET SALAD

A welcome time-saver—

Dissolve one 3-ounce package fruit-flavored gelatin in 1 cup boiling water. Add 8 to 12 ice cubes; stir constantly till gelatin starts to thicken, about 2 to 3 minutes. Remove unmelted ice. Let stand 3 to 5 minutes. Fold in fruits or vegetables; chill till firm.

SWEET APPLE RING

 1 cup apple juice
 1 3-ounce package lemon-flavored gelatin
 1 cup cold water
 ¼ teaspoon salt
 ½ cup diced unpared apple
 ¼ cup seedless green grapes
 1 8¾-ounce can pineapple tidbits, drained
 ½ cup miniature marshmallows

Heat apple juice to boiling; add to gelatin and stir till gelatin is dissolved. Stir in cold water and salt. Chill till partially set. Fold in remaining ingredients; pour into 4½-cup ring mold. Chill till firm. Serves 4 or 5.

PEAR SALAD RING

Cheese balls make a surprise pear center—

Drain one 29-ounce can pear halves, reserving syrup; add enough water to make 1¾ cups liquid. Dissolve two 3-ounce packages lemon-flavored gelatin in 2 cups boiling water. Stir in reserved pear syrup, 2 tablespoons lemon juice, ½ teaspoon ground ginger, and ¼ teaspoon salt. Chill gelatin mixture till partially set.

Meanwhile, form one 3-ounce package cream cheese, softened, into small balls to equal number of pear halves. Roll balls in ¼ cup chopped walnuts; place 1 ball in center of each pear half.

Pour about a *fourth* of the partially set gelatin into 6½-cup ring mold. Arrange pear halves, ball side down, and 8 thinly sliced green pepper strips (optional) on top of gelatin. Carefully pour remaining gelatin mixture over. Chill till firm. Serves 8.

HOLIDAY WREATH

- 1 8¾-ounce can seedless green grapes
- 1 3-ounce package lime-flavored gelatin
- ½ cup chopped celery
- 1 envelope (1 tablespoon) unflavored gelatin
- ½ cup frozen lemonade concentrate, thawed
- ½ cup mayonnaise or salad dressing
- 1 16-ounce can fruit cocktail
- 1 3-ounce package cherry-flavored gelatin
  Lemon Mayonnaise

Drain grapes, reserving syrup. Add enough water to syrup to make 1 cup. Dissolve lime-flavored gelatin in 1 cup boiling water; stir in syrup mixture. Chill till partially set. Fold in grapes and celery. Pour into 8½-cup ring mold; chill till *almost* firm. Soften unflavored gelatin in ½ cup cold water; stir over low heat till gelatin is dissolved. Add lemonade concentrate and 1 cup cold water; beat in mayonnaise. Chill till partially set. Pour over lime layer. Chill again till second layer is *almost* firm.

Drain fruit cocktail, reserving syrup. Add water to syrup to make 1 cup liquid. Dissolve cherry-flavored gelatin in 1 cup boiling water; stir in syrup mixture. Chill till partially set. Fold in fruit cocktail; pour over lemon layer. Chill till firm. Serve with Lemon Mayonnaise. Makes 12 to 14 servings.

Lemon Mayonnaise: Combine ½ cup mayonnaise or salad dressing and ¼ cup frozen lemonade concentrate, thawed. Fold in ½ cup whipping cream, whipped.

CRANBERRY WINE SALAD

A luscious mold for luncheons—

Dissolve two 3-ounce packages raspberry-flavored gelatin in 2 cups boiling water. Stir in one 16-ounce can whole cranberry sauce, one 8¾-ounce can undrained crushed pineapple, and ¾ cup port. Chill till partially set. Fold in ¼ cup chopped walnuts. Pour gelatin mixture into 6½-cup mold. Chill till firm. Makes 10 to 12 servings.

CREAMY PEAR-LIME MOLD

- 1 4-serving envelope low-calorie lime-flavored gelatin
- 1 3-ounce package Neufchatel cheese, softened
- 2 tablespoons skim milk
  . . .
- 1 16-ounce can dietetic-pack pear halves, drained and diced
- 1 medium banana, peeled and sliced

Prepare gelatin following package directions. Beat cheese with milk; slowly add gelatin, beating till light and fluffy. Chill till partially set. Fold in pears and banana. Pour into 4½-cup mold. Chill till firm. Serves 6.

APPLE-GRAPEFRUIT MOLDS

- 1 8-ounce can grapefruit sections
- 1 3-ounce package lime-flavored gelatin
- 1 cup diced unpared apple

Drain grapefruit, reserving syrup; cut up grapefruit sections. Dissolve gelatin in 1 cup boiling water. Add enough water to reserved syrup to make 1 cup; stir into dissolved gelatin. Chill till partially set.

Fold in grapefruit and apple. Pour into six ½-cup molds. Chill till firm. Serves 6.

CHEESE-NUT RING

- 1 3-ounce package lime-flavored gelatin
- 1 7-ounce bottle (about 1 cup) ginger ale, chilled
  . . .
- 1 12-ounce carton (1½ cups) small curd cream-style cottage cheese, *well* drained
- 1 tablespoon mayonnaise or salad dressing
- ¼ cup chopped pistachio nuts

Dissolve gelatin in 1 cup boiling water. Cool; gently stir in ginger ale. Chill till partially set. Combine remaining ingredients; fold into gelatin. Pour into 3½-cup mold. Chill till firm. Makes 4 to 6 servings.

CANTALOUPE CROWN

1 small cantaloupe
1 3-ounce package lemon-lime-
flavored gelatin
1 3-ounce package lime-flavored
gelatin
2½ cups boiling water
¼ cup lemon juice
Dash salt
1 7-ounce bottle (about 1 cup)
lemon-lime carbonated
beverage, chilled

Halve cantaloupe; remove seeds and rind. Cut in wedges about ¾ inch thick at the widest part. Dissolve lemon-lime- and lime-flavored gelatins in boiling water; stir in lemon juice and salt. Cool.

Pour carbonated beverage slowly down side of bowl into gelatin; stir gently to mix. Chill till partially set. Arrange cantaloupe in 6½-cup fluted tube mold. Carefully pour a *fourth* of the gelatin mixture into mold covering bottom of cantaloupe. Chill gelatin in mold till *almost* firm. Leave remaining gelatin at room temperature.

Slowly pour *half* of remaining gelatin mixture into mold; chill till *almost* firm. Pour remaining gelatin into mold; chill till firm. Before unmolding, trim off tips of cantaloupe wedges if extending above gelatin. Makes 8 servings.

APPLE-AVOCADO RING

Spiced apples zip up this two-layered mold—

Dissolve one 3-ounce package strawberry-flavored gelatin in 1 cup boiling water. Drain one 16-ounce jar spiced apple rings, reserving ¼ cup syrup. Add syrup and ¾ cup water to dissolved gelatin; chill till partially set. Dice apple rings, reserving 3 whole rings. Fold diced apple into gelatin. Pour into 6½-cup mold; chill till *almost* firm.

Dissolve one 3-ounce package lemon-flavored gelatin in 1 cup boiling water; add ½ cup cold water and 1 tablespoon lemon juice. Chill till partially set. Fold ½ cup whipping cream, whipped, and 2 avocados, peeled and mashed (1 cup), into lemon-flavored gelatin. Pour over apple layer. Chill till firm. Garnish with reserved apple rings. Makes 8 servings.

STRAWBERRY CUPS

Use fresh or frozen berries—

Drain one 8¾-ounce can pineapple tidbits, reserving ½ cup syrup. Combine 1 cup fresh strawberries, hulled and halved*, and 2 tablespoons sugar; chill till juice forms. Drain, reserving juice; heat to boiling with enough water to make 1¼ cups. Dissolve one 3-ounce package strawberry-flavored gelatin in boiling juice. Stir in reserved pineapple syrup, 2 tablespoons lemon juice, and dash salt. Chill till partially set. Fold in fruits. Pour into six ½-cup molds; chill till firm. Makes 6 servings.

*Or use two 10-ounce packages frozen sliced strawberries, thawed; drain, reserving 1 cup juice. Bring juice to boiling. Dissolve gelatin in boiling juice.

WINTER FRUIT SOUFFLE

1 3-ounce package lime-flavored
gelatin
½ cup mayonnaise or salad
dressing
1½ tablespoons lemon juice
2 tablespoons finely chopped
celery
1 16-ounce can grapefruit sections,
drained and diced
1 avocado, peeled and mashed

Dissolve gelatin in 1 cup boiling water. Add ½ cup cold water, mayonnaise, lemon juice, and ¼ teaspoon salt. Beat with rotary beater till smooth. Chill till partially set, then whip till fluffy. Fold in celery and fruit. Pour into 4½-cup mold; chill till firm. Serves 6.

HARVEST CREAM

Dissolve one 3-ounce package lemon-flavored gelatin in 1 cup apple juice heated to boiling. Stir in 1 cup cold apple juice. Chill till partially set. Add 1 cup chopped unpared apple and ¼ cup chopped pecans to *1 cup* gelatin. Pour into 5½-cup mold; chill till *almost* firm. Prepare one 2-ounce package dessert topping mix according to package directions; fold into remaining gelatin. Pour over first layer. Chill till firm. Serves 5 or 6.

ORANGE-APRICOT RING

       2 16-ounce cans apricot halves
       2 3-ounce packages orange-
          flavored gelatin
       1 6-ounce can frozen orange juice
          concentrate
       2 tablespoons lemon juice
       1 7-ounce bottle (about 1 cup)
          lemon-lime carbonated
          beverage, chilled

Drain apricots, reserving 1½ cups syrup. Puree apricots in sieve or blender. Heat reserved syrup to boiling; dissolve gelatin and dash salt in syrup. Add puree, juice concentrate, and lemon juice; stir till concentrate is melted. Slowly pour carbonated beverage down side of pan; mix gently. Pour gelatin mixture into 6½-cup ring mold. Chill till firm. Makes 10 to 12 servings.

HEAVENLY ORANGE FLUFF

       2 3-ounce packages orange-
          flavored gelatin
       1 13½-ounce can crushed pineapple
       1 6-ounce can frozen orange juice
          concentrate, thawed
       2 11-ounce cans mandarin oranges,
          drained
       1 3¾-ounce package *instant*
          lemon pudding mix
       1 cup cold milk
       1 cup whipping cream, whipped

Dissolve gelatin in 2½ cups boiling water; add undrained pineapple and concentrate. Chill till partially set. Fold in oranges; pour into 13x9x2-inch pan. Chill till firm. Beat pudding and milk with rotary beater till smooth. Fold in whipped cream. Spread over gelatin; chill. Makes 12 to 15 servings.

Green spinach leaves, crisp and fresh, nestle in the center of flaming Orange-apricot Ring while selected fruits—green grapes, plums, avocado, and pineapple—encircle it on a large serving platter. Have fun using artistic imagination to make every recipe a treat to eye and appetite.

SALADS THAT MELLOW IN TIME

CINNAMON FRUIT SALAD

Tiny cloud-like puffs of marshmallow enhance this creamy, cinnamon-flavored fruit salad—

- ¼ cup red cinnamon candies
- 2 tablespoons vinegar
- 2 tablespoons water
  Dash salt
- 3 beaten egg yolks
- 2 tablespoons honey
- 1 tablespoon butter or margarine
- 1 tablespoon lemon juice
- 2 cups sliced banana
- 3 cups diced unpared apple
- 1 cup miniature marshmallows
- 1 cup halved seedless green grapes
- ½ cup whipping cream, whipped

In small saucepan, combine first 4 ingredients. Cook and stir till candies are dissolved. In small bowl, combine egg yolks and honey. Gradually stir hot cinnamon mixture into egg yolk mixture; return to saucepan. Add butter. Cook and stir 3 to 4 minutes, or till thickened; cool. In large bowl, sprinkle lemon juice over banana; let stand a few minutes. Add apple, marshmallows, and grapes. Fold in cinnamon mixture and whipped cream. Chill several hours or overnight. Makes 10 to 12 servings.

5-CUP SALAD

A salad that's as easy as its name—

- 1 8¾-ounce can pineapple tidbits, drained (⅔ cup)
- 1 cup drained orange segments
- 1 cup shredded coconut
- 1 cup miniature marshmallows
- 1 cup dairy sour cream

Combine ingredients. Chill several hours or overnight. Makes 5 or 6 servings.

FRUIT GALAXY SALAD

- 1 8-ounce can dietetic-pack pineapple tidbits
- 1 tablespoon cornstarch
- 2 tablespoons lemon juice
  Non-caloric liquid sweetener equal to ¼ cup sugar
  . . .
- ½ cup plain yogurt
- 1 cup sliced fresh peaches
- 1 cup diced unpared apple
- ½ cup diced fresh pear
- ½ cup sliced banana
- ½ cup halved seedless green grapes

Drain pineapple tidbits, reserving ½ cup juice. In 1½-quart saucepan, gradually stir pineapple juice into cornstarch. Stir in lemon juice and sweetener. Cook and stir over medium heat till thickened and bubbly; cool. Fold in yogurt, then pineapple, peaches, apple, pear, banana, and grapes. Chill several hours. Makes 8 servings.

CRANBERRY-GRAPE SALAD

Either dessert or salad. Try both ways—

- 2 cups fresh cranberries
- ¾ cup sugar
  . . .
- 1 cup seeded halved red grapes
- ¼ cup broken walnuts
- 2 cups miniature marshmallows
- ½ cup whipping cream, whipped

Grind cranberries through food chopper, using coarse blade. Stir in sugar. Cover and chill overnight. Drain, pressing lightly to remove excess juice. Add grapes, nuts, and marshmallows to *well-drained* cranberry mixture. Just before serving, fold in whipped cream. Mound in lettuce cups. Garnish with grape clusters, if desired. Serves 6 to 8.

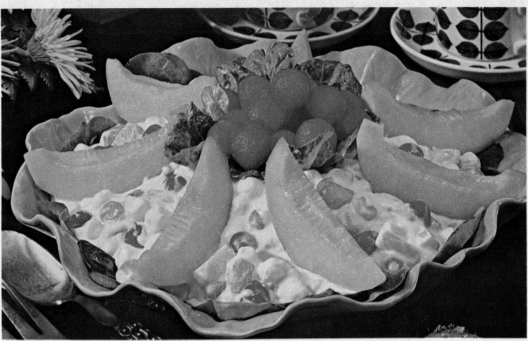

The delightful flavors in 24-hour Salad mingle as the fruits chill leisurely in a fluffy whipped cream dressing. It's a do-ahead salad and perfect for the buffet table. Pile on platter lined with greens and garnish with golden cantaloupe wedges and rosy watermelon balls.

24-HOUR SALAD

> 1 20½-ounce can pineapple tidbits
> 3 egg yolks
> 2 tablespoons sugar
> 2 tablespoons vinegar
> 1 tablespoon butter or margarine
> 1 16-ounce can pitted light
>   sweet cherries, drained
> 2 pared oranges, cut up and
>   drained
> ¼ cup drained maraschino cherries
> 2 cups miniature marshmallows
> 1 cup whipping cream, whipped

Drain pineapple, reserving 2 tablespoons syrup. In top of double boiler, beat egg yolks slightly; add reserved syrup, sugar, vinegar, butter, and dash salt. Place over *hot not boiling* water; cook, stirring constantly till mixture thickens *slightly* and *barely* coats a spoon (about 12 minutes). Cool to room temperature. Combine *well-drained* fruits and marshmallows. Pour custard over and mix gently. Fold in whipped cream. Turn into serving bowl. Cover and chill 24 hours. Serves 6 to 8.

CREAMY FRUIT COMBO

> 1 cup seedless green grapes
> 1 8¾-ounce can pineapple
>   tidbits, drained (⅔ cup)
> 1 cup pitted dark sweet cherries
> 1 cup diced orange
> 1 cup cantaloupe balls
> 2 medium plums, sliced
> ⅔ cup flaked coconut
>
> • • •
>
> Creamy Dressing
> 1 cup sliced banana

Combine first 7 ingredients. Fold in Creamy Dressing. Chill 24 hours to allow flavors to blend fully. Fold in sliced banana just before serving. Makes 8 to 10 servings.

Creamy Dressing: In small saucepan, combine 2 beaten eggs, 2 tablespoons orange juice, and 2 tablespoons vinegar; stir in ¼ cup sugar and dash salt. Cook over low heat, stirring constantly, till mixture thickens. Remove from heat and stir in 1 tablespoon butter or margarine. Cool. Fold in 1 cup dairy sour cream. Chill thoroughly.

SALADS FROM THE FREEZER

APPLE SNOW SALAD

In saucepan, combine one 8¾-ounce can undrained crushed pineapple, 2 beaten eggs, ½ cup sugar, ¼ cup water, 3 tablespoons lemon juice, and dash salt. Cook over low heat, stirring constantly, till thickened. Chill.

Stir in 2 cups diced unpared apple and ½ cup chopped walnuts; fold in 1 cup whipping cream, whipped. Pour into 8x8x2-inch pan. Freeze till firm. Let stand at room temperature 10 to 15 minutes before serving. Cut into squares. Makes 9 servings.

PINEAPPLE MINT FREEZE

1 20½-ounce can crushed
   pineapple
1 envelope (1 tablespoon)
   unflavored gelatin
1 10-ounce jar mint jelly
1 cup whipping cream
1 teaspoon confectioners' sugar

Drain pineapple, reserving syrup. In saucepan, soften gelatin in syrup. Add jelly and dash salt; heat and stir till gelatin is dissolved and jelly melted. If needed, beat to blend jelly. Stir in pineapple. Chill till mixture is thickened and syrupy.

Whip cream with sugar; fold into thickened gelatin mixture. Tint with few drops green food coloring, if desired. Spoon into 8½x4½x2½-inch loaf dish. Freeze till firm. Let stand at room temperature 10 to 15 minutes before serving. Unmold; slice and place on lettuce-lined salad plates. Garnish with fresh mint sprigs, if desired. Serves 8.

←Give the hot summer meal a cool lift by serving Pineapple Mint Freeze for the salad course. Fresh mint sprigs and ruffles of leaf lettuce spruce up this eye-catching, creamy refresher.

DATE-PECAN MOLDS

1 8-ounce package cream cheese,
   softened
¼ cup orange juice
1 8¾-ounce can crushed
   pineapple, drained (¾ cup)
½ cup snipped pitted dates
½ cup chopped pecans
¼ cup chopped maraschino cherries
½ teaspoon grated orange peel
1 cup whipping cream, whipped
8 orange slices (cut crosswise)

Beat together cream cheese and orange juice till fluffy. Stir in drained pineapple, dates, nuts, cherries, and orange peel. Fold in whipped cream. Spoon into eight ½-cup molds or one 8½x4½x2½-inch loaf dish. Freeze till firm. Let stand at room temperature 10 to 15 minutes before serving. Unmold each on orange slice. Serves 8.

BERRY-FRUIT FREEZE

2 3-ounce packages cream cheese,
   softened
2 tablespoons sugar
2 tablespoons mayonnaise or
   salad dressing
1 16-ounce can whole cranberry
   sauce
1 8¾-ounce can crushed
   pineapple, drained (¾ cup)
½ cup chopped walnuts
1 cup whipping cream, whipped
4 drops red food coloring

Beat cream cheese with sugar and mayonnaise. Stir in cranberry sauce, pineapple, and nuts. Fold in whipped cream and food coloring. Pour into 8½x4½x2½-inch loaf dish. Freeze till firm. Let stand at room temperature 10 to 15 minutes before serving. Unmold; slice to serve. Serves 8 to 10.

Quickest way to freeze salad mixture is in a freezer tray. To serve, cut in wedges or squares.

For round slices, pour mixture into No. 2 or 2½ can (20 to 29 ounce capacity). Freeze till firm.

To remove, let stand out a few minutes. Loosen end of can with opener; push out and slice.

SHORTCUT FROZEN SALAD

Prepare one 3⅝- or 3¾-ounce package *instant* lemon pudding mix according to package directions. Stir in 2 cups frozen dessert topping, thawed; ½ cup mayonnaise or salad dressing; and 2 tablespoons lemon juice. Fold in one 16-ounce can fruit cocktail, drained; 1 cup miniature marshmallows; and ¼ cup chopped pecans. Turn into 9x5x3-inch loaf pan. Freeze till firm. Serves 8 to 10.

CRAN-CHEESE FROSTIES

    1 16-ounce can jellied cranberry
        sauce
    2 tablespoons lemon juice
    1 3-ounce package cream cheese,
        softened
    ¼ cup mayonnaise or salad
        dressing
    ¼ cup sifted confectioners' sugar
    ¼ cup chopped walnuts
    1 cup whipping cream, whipped

Beat cranberry sauce and lemon juice till smooth. Pour into 6 to 8 paper baking cups, filling about ⅓ full *or* one 4-cup freezer tray. Beat together next 3 ingredients. Stir in walnuts. Fold in whipped cream and spread over cranberry layer. Freeze till firm. Serve on lettuce. Makes 6 to 8 servings.

RHUBARB FREEZE

A perfect summer special—

In small saucepan, combine 1 cup diced fresh rhubarb, 2 tablespoons water, and ¼ cup sugar. Cover and cook over medium heat about 3 minutes, or till rhubarb is tender, stirring occasionally; cool. Combine rhubarb and one 8¾-ounce can undrained crushed pineapple. Drain mixture, reserving ½ cup of the fruit juice.

Beat together one 8-ounce package cream cheese, softened; ¼ cup sugar; 1 tablespoon lemon juice; 7 drops red food coloring; and reserved juice. Stir in drained fruit and 1 cup miniature marshmallows. Fold 1 cup whipping cream, whipped, into fruit mixture. Pour into eight to ten ½-cup molds. Freeze till firm. Makes 8 to 10 servings.

Keep Cranberry-orange Salad in mind for an extra-easy salad. The flavor combination makes it especially suitable for holiday meals consisting of turkey and all the trimmings. Line the salad plates with crisp leaf lettuce, then garnish each square with a frosty cluster of red grapes.

CRANBERRY-ORANGE SALAD

  1 3¾-ounce package vanilla
      whipped dessert mix
½ cup ginger ale
      •   •   •
  1 cup cranberry-orange relish
    Leaf lettuce
    Frosted red grape clusters

Prepare vanilla whipped dessert mix according to package directions, substituting the ½ cup ginger ale for the recommended amount of water in package directions.

Fold cranberry-orange relish into dessert mixture. Pour into 8x8x2-inch pan. Freeze till firm. To serve salad, cut in squares. Place on leaf lettuce-lined plates. Garnish with clusters of frosted red grapes (see Index). Makes 6 servings.

CRANBERRY BANANA LOAF

An unusual blend of fruit flavors—

  1 16-ounce can jellied cranberry
      sauce
  1 medium apple, pared and grated
  2 medium bananas, mashed
⅓ cup sifted confectioners' sugar
  1 teaspoon vanilla
¼ cup chopped walnuts
  1 cup whipping cream, whipped

Beat cranberry sauce till smooth; stir in grated apple. Pour into 11x7x1½-inch pan. Fold bananas, sugar, vanilla, and *half* the nuts into whipped cream. Spread over cranberry layer. Sprinkle with remaining nuts. Freeze till firm. Let stand at room temperature 15 minutes; cut in squares. Serves 8.

FRUIT MEAL-MAKERS

GLAZED AVOCADO BOATS

An enticing aroma abounds from this salad—

- 1 8¾-ounce can pineapple tidbits
- 1 *teaspoon* unflavored gelatin
- 1 tablespoon sugar
- ¼ teaspoon grated lime peel
- 1 tablespoon lime juice
- 1 medium unpared apple, diced
- 1 orange, pared and diced
- ½ cup diced celery
- 3 medium avocados

Drain pineapple, reserving syrup. Combine gelatin, sugar, and dash salt. Heat syrup and ½ cup water to boiling; add to gelatin mixture and stir till gelatin and sugar are dissolved. Stir in lime peel and juice. Chill till partially set. Combine pineapple tidbits, apple, orange, and celery. Halve avocados lengthwise; remove seeds and skin. Place one half on each of 6 lettuce-lined luncheon plates. Spoon fruit into cavities. Drizzle gelatin over. Makes 6 servings.

FRUIT AND CHEESE PLATE

- 1 30-ounce can pineapple slices
- 1 3-ounce package orange-flavored gelatin
- 1 3-ounce package cream cheese, cubed and softened
- ¼ cup orange juice
- 1 tablespoon lemon juice
- 1 16-ounce carton (2 cups) cream-style cottage cheese

Drain pineapple, reserving syrup. Halve pineapple slices; set aside. Add water to syrup to make 1½ cups. Bring to boiling; add to gelatin and stir till dissolved. With rotary beater, gradually beat hot gelatin into cheese. Stir in juices. Chill till partially set, stirring occasionally. Pour into four ½-cup molds. Chill till firm. Unmold; arrange on 4 lettuce-lined plates with pineapple and cottage cheese. Makes 4 servings.

PAPAYA FRUIT SALAD

Cut 1 large papaya into eighths; remove seeds and membrane. Pare and section 2 medium grapefruit. Peel and slice 2 medium bananas*. Center a generous scoop of lime sherbet on each of 4 lettuce-lined luncheon plates. Arrange papaya, grapefruit, bananas, and 1 cup halved and seeded red grapes around edge. Makes 4 servings.

*To keep bananas bright, use ascorbic acid color keeper or dip in lemon juice mixed with a little water.

FRUITED PARFAIT SALAD

- 1 16-ounce package frozen sliced strawberries
- 1 10-ounce package frozen melon balls *or* 1 cup fresh melon balls
- 1 10-ounce package frozen blueberries *or* 1 cup fresh blueberries
- 1 cup dairy sour cream
- ½ teaspoon grated lemon peel
- 1 16-ounce carton (2 cups) large curd cream-style cottage cheese

Partially thaw and drain frozen fruits separately, reserving ¼ cup strawberry syrup. Prepare dressing by blending together sour cream, reserved syrup, and lemon peel.

Allowing ⅓ cup cottage cheese for each salad, begin layering with *half* the cottage cheese in bottoms of 6 large parfait glasses. Continue layering with dressing, strawberries, a few melon balls, blueberries, remaining cottage cheese, dressing, and strawberries. Top with remaining melon balls. Serve immediately. Makes 6 servings.

Choose Fruited Parfait Salad to be the dazzling attraction at a forthcoming luncheon. There's versatility in this recipe since fresh or frozen fruits can be used depending on their availability.

POLYNESIAN SALAD

LOW CALORIE · LOW CALORIE

1 large cantaloupe
6 heads Bibb lettuce
1 14-ounce can dietetic-pack
   pineapple slices, drained and
   halved
1 medium papaya, peeled and
   thinly sliced
2 medium peaches, peeled and
   thinly sliced*
2 medium plums, thinly sliced
1 medium unpared apple, thinly
   sliced*
2 cups fresh whole strawberries

Chill all fruits and lettuce thoroughly. Cut midsection of cantaloupe into 6 rings. Remove seeds and rind. Remove rind from end pieces of cantaloupe and cut into thin spears. Cut roots from heads of Bibb lettuce leaving heads in one piece.

To assemble salads, spread Bibb leaves apart. Place 1 cantaloupe ring on each of 6 luncheon plates. Top each with a head of lettuce. Tuck slices or spears of the different fruits on end among the Bibb leaves. Fill in with hulled strawberries. Serve with a low-calorie dressing (see Index). Serves 6.

LUNCHEON SALAD

1 20½-ounce can pineapple chunks
2 12-ounce cartons (3 cups)
   cream-style cottage cheese
1 cup halved pitted dark sweet
   cherries
3 oranges, peeled and sectioned
1 banana, peeled and cut in
   sixths*
1 cup halved seedless green
   grapes
 • • •
½ cup mayonnaise or salad
   dressing
½ cup whipping cream, whipped

Drain pineapple, reserving ½ cup syrup. Arrange pineapple, cottage cheese, cherries, oranges, banana, and grapes on lettuce-lined plates. Prepare dressing by folding reserved syrup and mayonnaise into whipped cream. Chill salads and dressing separately. At serving time, pass dressing. Makes 6 servings.

APRICOT-CHEESE SALAD

1 30-ounce can apricot halves
1 8¾-ounce can crushed
   pineapple
1 3-ounce package orange-
   flavored gelatin
1 12-ounce carton (1½ cups)
   cream-style cottage cheese
2 tablespoons all-purpose flour
2 tablespoons sugar
1 slightly beaten egg
1 tablespoon butter or margarine
1 cup frozen whipped dessert
   topping, thawed
⅓ cup shredded sharp process
   American cheese
3 bananas, peeled and bias-cut*
   Grape clusters

Drain apricots and pineapple, reserving ½ cup combined syrups. Dissolve gelatin in 1 cup boiling water; stir in 1 cup cold water. Chill till partially set. Fold in pineapple and cottage cheese. Pour into six ½-cup molds; chill till gelatin mixture is firm.

In small saucepan, combine flour and sugar. Stir in reserved syrup; blend in egg. Cook and stir till thickened. Remove from heat; stir in butter. Place clear plastic wrap or waxed paper directly on dressing; cool. Peel off covering. Fold in thawed dessert topping and American cheese.

At serving time, unmold gelatin salads in center of lettuce-lined plates. Arrange bananas and drained apricots around molds. Garnish with grape clusters. Pass cooked dressing. Makes 6 servings.

BERRY-PATCH SALAD

2 medium cantaloupes, chilled
1 12-ounce carton (1½ cups)
   cream-style cottage cheese
1 8¾-ounce can pineapple
   tidbits, chilled and drained
½ cup hulled and halved fresh
   strawberries
½ cup fresh red raspberries

Cut cantaloupes in half crosswise; remove seeds. Combine cottage cheese and pineapple. Spoon into melon halves. Top with strawberries and raspberries. Serves 4.

Any one of 3 cantaloupe-based salads makes a colorful mid-summer meal. Peaches and blueberries wreath lime sherbet for a Luncheon Cooler.

Coronado Salad boasts a liberally-garnished chicken salad. Red berries couched in a fruited cottage cheese bed spark the Berry-patch Salad.

CORONADO SALAD

  2 medium cantaloupes, chilled
  2 cups diced cooked chicken
  ½ cup chopped celery
  ½ cup halved seedless green
     grapes
  2 tablespoons sliced pimiento-
     stuffed green olives
  ½ teaspoon monosodium
     glutamate
  ½ cup whipping cream, whipped
  ¼ cup mayonnaise
  4 clusters seedless green grapes
    Hard-cooked egg slices
    Toasted sliced almonds

Cut cantaloupes in half crosswise; remove seeds. Combine next 5 ingredients and ½ teaspoon salt reserving a few olive slices; toss. Fold in mixture of whipped cream and mayonnaise. Spoon into melons. Garnish with remaining ingredients. Serves 4.

LUNCHEON COOLER

  2 medium cantaloupes, chilled
  2 medium peaches, peeled
  2 bananas, peeled and sliced*
  ½ cup fresh blueberries
  3 tablespoons honey
  2 to 3 teaspoons finely snipped
     candied ginger
    Lime sherbet

Cut cantaloupes in half crosswise; remove seeds. Slice *one* peach* and reserve for garnish. Dice remaining peach* into large bowl. Add next 4 ingredients and toss lightly; spoon into cantaloupe halves. Arrange reserved peaches around each cantaloupe rim; top with a scoop of lime sherbet. Garnish with extra blueberries, if desired. Serves 4.

*To keep fruit attractive and bright, dip in ascorbic acid color keeper or dip in lemon juice mixed with a little water.

BUFFET SPECIALS

BUFFET FRUIT BOWL

1 large banana
2 fresh medium pears
1 large apple
1 medium pink grapefruit
1 3-ounce package cream cheese, softened
2 ounces (½ cup) blue cheese, softened
½ cup chopped pecans
4 canned peach halves
Green grape clusters
Romaine
Cranberry-orange relish
Honey-lime Dressing
Creamy Poppy Seed Dressing
Chutney French Dressing

Peel banana and score lengthwise with tines of fork; cut diagonally into crosswise sections*. Halve pears*; remove cores. Cut apple into wedges*; remove core. Peel and section grapefruit. Blend cream cheese and blue cheese. Form into balls; roll in nuts.

Arrange fruits on bed of romaine in salad bowl. Top pears with cheese balls. Serve extra cheese balls on the side. Spoon relish into peaches. Serve with Honey-lime Dressing, Creamy Poppy Seed Dressing, and Chutney French Dressing. Makes 6 servings.

Honey-lime Dressing: In saucepan, combine 1 beaten egg, ½ cup honey, and ¼ cup lime juice. Cook and stir over low heat till mixture thickens. Blend in dash *each* salt and ground mace; cool. Fold in 1 cup dairy sour cream. Chill. Makes 1½ cups.

Creamy Poppy Seed Dressing: In mixing bowl, combine ½ cup mayonnaise or salad dressing, 2 tablespoons sugar, and 1 tablespoon lemon juice; blend thoroughly. Stir in 1 tablespoon poppy seed. Makes about ¾ cup.

Chutney French Dressing: In screw-top jar, combine 1 cup sweet French salad dressing, 2 tablespoons finely chopped chutney, and 1 teaspoon grated orange peel. Cover and shake well. Chill. Makes about 1 cup.

*To keep fruits bright, use ascorbic acid color keeper or dip in lemon juice mixed with a little water.

PINEAPPLE-TOP LAYERS

A colorful ribbon highlights a Christmas meal—

1 3-ounce package lime-flavored gelatin
1 cup boiling water
1 13½-ounce can pineapple chunks
2 tablespoons lemon juice
1 3-ounce package lemon-flavored gelatin
1 cup boiling water
2 3-ounce packages cream cheese, softened
⅓ cup mayonnaise or salad dressing
1 3-ounce package raspberry-flavored gelatin
1 cup boiling water
2 medium bananas, peeled and sliced (2 cups)

Dissolve lime-flavored gelatin in the *first* 1 cup boiling water. Drain pineapple, reserving syrup. Add lemon juice and enough water to syrup to make 1 cup; stir into gelatin mixture. Chill till partially set. Fold in pineapple chunks. Pour into one 10½-cup mold. Chill till *almost* firm.

Dissolve lemon-flavored gelatin in the *second* 1 cup boiling water. Chill till partially set. Whip gelatin mixture till light and the consistency of whipped cream. Beat cream cheese and mayonnaise together till smooth. Gradually fold whipped gelatin into cheese mixture. Pour over first layer. Chill lemon layer till *almost* firm.

Dissolve raspberry-flavored gelatin in the *third* 1 cup boiling water. Stir 1 cup cold water into gelatin mixture. Chill till partially set. Arrange banana slices over almost firm lemon layer; pour gelatin over. Chill till firm. Makes 10 to 12 servings.

Fruit arrangements make a flavorful addition →
to a buffet dinner. Combining fresh and canned fruits, Buffet Fruit Bowl is served with a complementary dressing assortment to please any taste.

PREPARING FOR A CROWD

Use this table as a guide when planning and shopping for food for a large group. The size of *one serving* (serving unit) has been listed for each item. For hearty eaters, plan approximately 1½ servings per person. Add accordingly for second helpings.

Food	Number of Servings	Serving Unit	Amount Needed
Beverages			
Coffee	25	1 cup	½ to ¾ pound
Tea, hot	25	1 cup	1 ounce
Tea, iced	25	1 glass	3 ounces
Cream, coffee	25	1 tablespoon	1 pint
Milk	24	1 8-ounce glass	1½ gallons
Breads			
Biscuits	25	2 ounces	4½ dozen
Bread	25	1-ounce slice	1¼ pounds
Rolls	24	1	2 dozen
Casseroles	25	1 cup	6¼ quarts
Desserts			
Cake	24	1/12 cake	2 9-inch layer cakes
	24	2½-inch square	1 15½x10½x1-inch sheet
Ice Cream	24	½ cup or 1 slice	3 quarts
Pie	30	1/6 pie	5 9-inch pies
Fruit			
Canned	24	½ cup	1 6½- to 7¼-pound can
Relishes			
Carrot strips	25	2 to 3 strips	1 to 1¼ pounds
Cauliflowerets	25	2 ounces sliced, raw	7 pounds
Celery	25	1 2- to 3-inch piece	1 medium stalk
Olives	25	3 to 4	1 quart
Pickles	25	1 ounce	1 quart
Radishes	25	2	5 bunches
Tomatoes	25	3 ounces, sliced	5 to 6¼ pounds
Salads			
Side Dish:			
Cottage cheese	25	⅓ cup	5 pounds
Fruit	24	⅓ cup	2 quarts
Gelatin	25	½ cup liquid	3 quarts
Potato	24	½ cup	3 quarts
Tossed vegetable	25	¾ cup	1¼ gallons
Main Dish	25	1 cup	6¼ quarts
Vegetables			
Canned	25	½ cup	1 6½- to 7¼-pound can
Fresh:			
Potatoes	25	½ cup, mashed	6¾ pounds
	25	1 medium, baked	8½ pounds
Frozen:			
Beans	25	⅓ cup	5¼ pounds
Carrots or peas	25	⅓ cup	5 pounds
Potatoes, French-fried	25	10 pieces	3¼ pounds

DELLA ROBBIA WREATH

Named after Luca della Robbia, a 15th century artist famous for ornamental wreaths—

2 16-ounce cans pear halves
1 29-ounce can peach halves
1 20-ounce can pineapple slices, halved
1 16-ounce can peeled whole apricots
1 16-ounce jar spiced crab apples

. . .

Salad greens
Seedless green grapes
Dairy sour cream

Chill fruit. Drain canned fruit and crab apples thoroughly, reserving syrup for salad dressing. Put pear halves together and peach halves together to resemble whole fruit. (If desired, spread a little softened cream cheese on cut sides of pear and peach halves to make them hold together.)

Arrange bed of greens on large round platter. Around outer rim place 2 pineapple halves, standing with cut side down, between each whole pear and peach. Arrange apricots and crab apples alternately to form an inner circle. Place seedless green grapes in center of platter; if desired, garnish fruit with watercress. To prepare salad dressing, thin sour cream with a little of the reserved syrup. Serve with fruit. Makes 10 to 12 servings.

MELON BASKET

Chill 1 honeydew melon, fresh raspberries, seedless green grapes, red grapes, purple grapes, and fresh plums. Pare chilled *whole* honeydew melon. Leaving about a 2-inch circle uncut at top and bottom, mark melon with wooden picks in 10 to 12 equal wedges. Remove every other wedge with knife. Discard seeds. Cut thin slice from one end of melon to make it sit flat. Stand basket, on cut surface, in center of large platter. Arrange melon wedges spoke fashion on platter opposite openings in basket. Tuck lemon wedges between melon wedges.

Fill hollow of basket with raspberries and top basket with mint sprigs. Arrange small bunches of grapes and plums around melon. Offer a choice of salad dressings.

SUMMER FRUIT PLATTER

Whole fresh pineapple
Apples
Fresh pears
Fresh strawberries, sliced
Oranges, sliced crosswise
Cantaloupe wedges
Stewed prunes, drained
Lime Honey *or* Marshmallow Blizzard

Chill fruit. Halve pineapple lengthwise; remove hard core. Scoop out fruit and cut into chunks. Cube apples and pears; toss with pineapple and strawberries. Pile fruit mixture into pineapple shells. Arrange on a tray with orange slices, cantaloupe wedges, and prunes. If desired, garnish with sprigs of mint. Serve with Lime Honey *or* Marshmallow Blizzard Dressing.

Lime Honey: Blend together ¼ cup honey with 2 tablespoons lime juice. Add dash salt.

Marshmallow Blizzard: To half of 7-ounce jar marshmallow creme, add 1 tablespoon *each* orange juice and lemon juice. With electric or rotary beater, beat till very fluffy. Fold in ¼ cup mayonnaise or salad dressing.

PARADE OF FRUIT TRAY

Pear Surprises
Canned whole apricots
Pineapple rings
Stewed prunes
Preserved kumquats
Canned peach halves
Cranberry-orange relish
Frosted grapes (see Index)
Spiced crab apples
Salad greens

Pear Surprises: Drain chilled canned pear halves. Pat dry with paper toweling. Fill hollow of each with cream cheese. Put a red cherry, pitted date, or fig in between two pear halves. Seal halves of pears together with softened cream cheese. Using pastry tube, pipe cream-cheese ruffle along edges.

Chill all fruit, then drain canned and stewed fruit. On bed of salad greens, arrange pears, apricots, pineapple, prunes, kumquats, peach halves filled with cranberry-orange relish, grapes, and crab apples.

ROSY-WREATHED HONEYDEW

Each dainty raspberry mold hides a tasty cream cheese and nut ball—

    1 20½-ounce can pineapple slices
    1 16-ounce can fruit cocktail
    1 3-ounce package raspberry-
        flavored gelatin
    3 tablespoons lemon juice
    1 3-ounce package cream cheese
    ¼ cup finely chopped walnuts
            . . .
        Honeydew Bowl
        Lettuce

Drain pineapple and fruit cocktail, reserving syrups. Add enough water to combined syrups to make 2 cups. Heat *1 cup* syrup mixture to boiling; add to gelatin and stir till gelatin is dissolved. Stir in remaining syrup mixture and lemon juice; chill gelatin mixture till partially set. Fold in drained fruit cocktail.

Form cream cheese into 8 balls; roll each in finely chopped nuts. Place 1 cheese ball in bottom of each of eight ½-cup molds. Carefully pour partially set gelatin over cheese balls in molds. Chill till firm.

Place Honeydew Bowl in center of large lettuce-lined platter. Arrange 8 pineapple slices on platter around Honeydew Bowl. Unmold individual raspberry molds on pineapple slices. Pass mayonnaise, if desired. Makes 8 servings.

Honeydew Bowl: Cut thin slice off bottom of 1 large honeydew, chilled, to make it sit flat. Cut top fourth off honeydew. Scoop out seeds and remove rind from entire melon. With round biscuit cutter, cut deep scallops around top edge of melon holding bottom of a custard cup or glass against inside of melon as each scallop is being cut.

Cube honeydew cut from scallops and top. Combine with drained canned peach and pear slices; remaining pineapple slices, cut in chunks; and seedless green grapes. Fill melon with fruit mixture. Trim with maraschino cherries and mint sprigs.

← **Lavishly displayed Fruited Watermelon** stars at an outdoor buffet. Heap juicy watermelon, cantaloupe, and honeydew balls in the cavity of the melon bowl and garnish with fresh fruit.

PEACH-PINEAPPLE RING

A fruit design arranged in the gelatin makes an impressive presentation—

    3 3-ounce packages lemon-flavored
        gelatin
    2 cups boiling water
    1 29-ounce can peach halves
    1 30-ounce can pineapple slices
    ½ cup drained maraschino
        cherries (20)

Dissolve gelatin in boiling water. Drain peaches and pineapple, reserving syrups. Combine syrups and add enough cold water to make 3 cups. Add syrup mixture to dissolved gelatin. Chill till partially set.

Alternate peaches, cut side up, and some of the cherries in bottom of 12½-cup ring mold. Gently pour *2 cups* partially set gelatin over; chill till *almost* firm. Keep remaining gelatin at room temperature. Halve pineapple slices; place, cut edge down, around outside and inside of mold to make "scalloped" design. Center remaining cherries in half rings. Carefully pour remaining gelatin over. Chill till firm. Makes 12 to 16 servings.

FRUITED WATERMELON

    1 large round watermelon
        Honeydew balls
        Cantaloupe balls
        Fresh blueberries
        Fresh raspberries
        Mint sprigs
        Red grape clusters
        Seedless green grape clusters
        Whole fresh plums
        Whole fresh pears

Cut slice off bottom of watermelon to make it sit flat. Cut top third off melon. Using a small bowl as guide, trace scallops around top edge. Carve out scallops following pattern; scoop out fruit. Place melon bowl on large platter. Cut watermelon fruit into balls with melon ball cutter. Chill all fruit.

Fill bowl with watermelon, honeydew, and cantaloupe balls. Top with blueberries and raspberries. Garnish with mint sprigs. Arrange grapes on platter around bottom of bowl. Fill in with plums and pears.

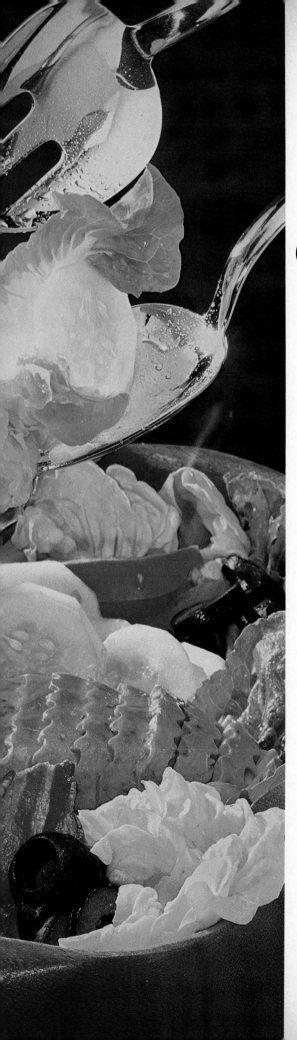

GARDEN-FRESH VEGETABLE SALADS

There is more to a good vegetable salad than lettuce and tomato. A myriad of greens and vegetables appear in salad bowls or gelatin molds.

For the tossed salad enthusiast there are ideas and recipes for basic and exotic combinations. And note, too, the Tips for Tossing that help the homemaker make the salad good to look at as well as good to eat.

There are many salad variations included in this chapter. Discover how gelatin, coleslaw, potato, macaroni, bean, and mixed vegetables build a salad recipe repertoire.

The chapter finale presents buffet salads with a vegetable twist—tossed, arranged, and molded.

The picturesque appeal of Superb Salad, a crackling-crisp tossed salad combination, is indicative of the tasteful and appealing recipes found in the following chapter.

GREEN SALAD TOSS-UPS

SUPERB SALAD

1 head romaine
1 head Bibb lettuce
1 small head lettuce
½ cup shredded Parmesan cheese
2 ounces blue cheese,
  crumbled (½ cup)
3 medium avocados

. . .

1 large cucumber, pared and
  sliced (1½ cups)
18 cherry tomatoes, halved
6 slices bacon, halved, crisp-
  cooked, and drained
  Red and green pepper slices
½ cup sliced pitted ripe olives
  Italian salad dressing

Tear salad greens into bite-size pieces; combine in large salad bowl. Sprinkle cheeses over greens. Halve avocados; remove seeds and peel. Slice avocado halves crosswise with fluted vegetable cutter. Arrange avocado slices, cucumber, tomatoes, bacon, pepper slices, and olives atop salad. To serve pour Italian salad dressing over vegetable mixture; toss lightly. Makes 12 to 14 servings.

DUTCH LETTUCE

5 slices bacon, diced
1 beaten egg
⅓ cup vinegar
¼ cup minced onion
2 tablespoons sugar
2 tablespoons water
6 cups torn leaf lettuce

In skillet, cook bacon till crisp. Do *not* drain. Combine egg, vinegar, onion, sugar, water, and ½ teaspoon salt; add to bacon and drippings. Heat just to boiling, stirring constantly. Place lettuce in bowl. Pour hot dressing over and toss lightly. Makes 6 servings.

HEARTS-OF-PALM SALAD

Pinch dried tarragon leaves,
  crushed
Pinch dried thyme leaves,
  crushed
Pinch dried basil leaves,
  crushed
2 tablespoons vinegar
⅓ cup olive *or* salad oil
1 tablespoon Dijon-style mustard
1 clove garlic, crushed
1 14-ounce can hearts of
  palm, drained
3 cups watercress
2 cups torn romaine
1 cup torn lettuce

To prepare dressing, soak tarragon, thyme, and basil in vinegar for 1 hour in screw-top jar. Dissolve ½ teaspoon salt in vinegar mixture. Add oil, mustard, garlic, and ½ teaspoon pepper. Shake well.

Cut hearts of palm in serving-size pieces; combine with watercress, romaine, and lettuce in large salad bowl. Pour dressing over; toss lightly. Makes 6 to 8 servings.

SUMMER SALAD BOWL

The enticing salad on the cover—

Leaf lettuce
4 cups torn lettuce
2 cups sliced raw cauliflower
1 cup bias-cut celery
1 cup sliced radishes
1 green pepper, thinly sliced
⅓ cup crumbled blue cheese
  Italian salad dressing

Line salad bowl with leaf lettuce. Arrange lettuce, cauliflower, celery, radishes, and green pepper in bowl. Sprinkle cheese over. Serve with Italian dressing. Serves 8 to 10.

TOSSED ARTICHOKE SALAD

½ cup salad oil
⅓ cup vinegar
4 thin slices onion
1 tablespoon sugar
1 clove garlic, crushed
¼ teaspoon celery seed
1 9-ounce package frozen
    artichoke hearts
1 4-ounce can pimientos,
    drained and chopped
2 cups *each* torn lettuce, torn
    romaine, and torn spinach

In saucepan, combine oil, vinegar, 2 table-spoons water, onion, sugar, garlic, ½ tea-spoon salt, celery seed, and dash pepper. Bring to boiling; add artichoke hearts. Cook till tender, 3 to 5 minutes; cool. Stir in pimiento. Chill. At serving time, drain re-serving marinade. In bowl, add artichoke mixture to torn salad greens. Toss with enough of reserved marinade (about ¼ cup) to coat greens. Makes 8 to 10 servings.

FAMILY GREEN SALAD

LOW CALORIE · LOW CALORIE ·

2 cups torn lettuce
2 cups torn curly endive
2 medium tomatoes, cut in wedges
½ medium green pepper, sliced
½ cup sliced celery
¼ cup sliced radishes
2 tablespoons chopped green onion
    Low-calorie French-style salad
    dressing

Place lettuce and endive in salad bowl. Ar-range next 5 ingredients over. Serve with low-calorie French-style dressing. Serves 6.

SPINACH-LETTUCE TOSS

In skillet, cook 5 slices bacon till crisp; drain, reserving drippings. Crumble bacon; combine with 3 cups *each* torn leaf lettuce and torn fresh spinach, ¼ cup diced celery, 2 tablespoons crumbled blue cheese, and 1 tablespoon chopped green onion. To drip-pings, add ¼ cup vinegar, 2 tablespoons sug-ar, and ½ teaspoon Worcestershire sauce; bring to boiling. Toss with salad. Serves 6.

SALATA

Means "mixed salad"—

6 cups shredded lettuce
3 tomatoes, peeled and chopped
1 large unpared cucumber,
    chopped
1 bunch watercress, chopped
1 medium green pepper, chopped
4 green onions, finely chopped
¼ cup sliced pitted Greek *or* ripe
    olives
3 tablespoons lemon juice
1 teaspoon salt
⅓ cup olive *or* salad oil

Combine first 6 ingredients. Add olives, lem-on juice, and salt; toss. Mound salad on platter. Garnish with additional tomato wedges, cucumber slices, and olives, if de-sired. Pour oil over all. Let stand 15 minutes to blend flavors. Serves 8 to 10.

HARVEST TOSS

In screw-top jar, combine 3 tablespoons salad oil, 2 tablespoons vinegar, 1½ tea-spoons sugar, ½ teaspoon salt, and dash pepper; shake well. In bowl, toss 6 cups torn leaf lettuce; 2 cups coarsely chopped unpared red apple; 1 cup thinly sliced unpared raw zucchini; and 1 small green pepper, cut in thin strips. Pour dressing over; toss. Serves 6.

CROUTONS FOR SALADS

Bread: Without removing crusts, cut white, whole wheat, or rye bread slices into small cubes. Toast cubes on baking sheet in slow oven (300°), stirring frequently, till dry and golden brown. In skillet, melt butter with 1 clove garlic. Remove garlic when it is golden brown. Add bread cubes; toss till they are butter coated.

Store a supply of croutons in a covered jar in the refrigerator. Heat them just before sprinkling over salads.

Walnut: In skillet, melt 2 tablespoons but-ter; add ½ teaspoon salt *or* garlic salt. Stir in ½ cup coarsely broken walnuts; brown over medium heat, stirring constantly. Add to salad dressing just before tossing.

BOSTON-COTTAGE TOSS

6 cups torn Boston *or* bibb
   lettuce
1 cup small curd cream-style
   cottage cheese
1 medium avocado, peeled and
   diced
⅓ cup coarsely chopped dill pickle
2 tablespoons sliced green onion
1 tablespoon salad oil
1 tablespoon wine vinegar
2 hard-cooked eggs, sliced

In large bowl season lettuce with salt and pepper; add next 4 ingredients. Toss in oil and vinegar; garnish with egg. Serves 4.

WILTED LETTUCE TOSS

4 slices bacon
4 cups torn leaf lettuce
1 large tomato, chopped
¼ cup sliced green onion
• • •
2 tablespoons vinegar
½ teaspoon dried oregano leaves,
   crushed

Fry bacon in large skillet till crisp; drain, reserving 1 tablespoon bacon drippings. Crumble bacon and set aside. Meanwhile, combine lettuce, tomato, and onion.

In skillet, heat reserved drippings, vinegar, oregano, ¼ teaspoon salt, and dash pepper to boiling. Gradually add lettuce mixture, tossing just till leaves are coated and wilted slightly. Turn into serving bowl. Top with crumbled bacon. Serve immediately. Makes 4 or 5 servings.

CHIFFONADE SALAD

• LOW CALORIE • LOW CALORIE •

Place four 1-inch slices lettuce on salad plates. For each salad, top lettuce with 1 tablespoon low-calorie French-style salad dressing. Arrange down center 1 tablespoon finely chopped canned or cooked beets, chilled. Finely chop 2 chilled hard-cooked eggs. Sprinkle ½ egg on each salad arranging on both sides of beets. Border each salad with 1 tablespoon finely chopped celery. Season. Pass extra dressing. Serves 4.

MODERN CAESAR SALAD

½ cup salad oil
¼ cup red wine vinegar
1 large clove garlic, crushed
2 teaspoons Worcestershire sauce
¼ teaspoon salt
   Dash pepper
3 slices bread, cubed
½ cup shredded Parmesan cheese
1 ounce blue cheese,
   crumbled (¼ cup)
8 cups torn romaine (about
   1 medium head)
1 egg

For dressing, shake together salad oil, red wine vinegar, crushed garlic, Worcestershire sauce, salt, and pepper in screw-top jar. Refrigerate a few hours or overnight to blend flavors. Toast bread cubes in slow oven (225°) for 2 hours.

To serve, sprinkle cheeses over romaine in salad bowl; add toasted bread cubes. Shake egg well with dressing; toss lightly with salad. Makes 6 to 8 servings.

PEPPERONI SALAD

6 cups torn lettuce (about 1
   medium head)
2 tomatoes, cut in wedges
4 ounces mozzarella cheese, cubed
   (1 cup)
1 cup drained garbanzo beans
½ cup thinly sliced pepperoni
¼ cup sliced green onion
½ cup Italian salad dressing
   Salt
   Freshly ground black pepper

In large salad bowl, combine lettuce, tomato wedges, cheese, garbanzo beans, pepperoni, and green onion. Pour Italian salad dressing over. Toss lettuce mixture lightly with dressing. Sprinkle with salt and pepper to taste. Makes 8 or 9 servings.

A taste of Italy comes through Pepperoni Salad. ➜ Sliced pepperoni, cubes of mozzarella cheese, garbanzo beans, and Italian dressing are tossed with crisp lettuce, juicy tomatoes, and green onion.

BACON AND TOMATO SALAD

A bacon-lettuce-tomato combo in a new form—

Toast 1 cup ½-inch bread cubes at 225° till dry, about 2 hours. Line salad bowl with romaine. Combine in salad bowl toasted bread cubes; 3 cups torn lettuce (½ medium head); 3 medium tomatoes, cut in wedges; 8 slices bacon, crisp-cooked and crumbled; and ½ cup mayonnaise or salad dressing. Toss lightly. Season to taste. Serves 4 or 5.

CHEF'S BOWL

1 clove garlic
1 medium head lettuce
. . .
1 to 2 cups fully-cooked ham cut in strips
1 8-ounce package process American cheese, cut in strips
1 pound fresh asparagus, cooked, drained, and chilled
1 10-ounce package frozen peas, cooked, drained, and chilled
¾ cup sliced radishes
Chef's French Dressing

Rub individual salad bowls with a cut end of garlic clove, then line with lettuce. Arrange next 5 ingredients in bowls. Season to taste with salt and pepper. Pass Chef's French Dressing. Makes 6 servings.

Chef's French Dressing: In screw-top jar, shake 2 tablespoons sugar and 1 teaspoon *each* salt, dry mustard, and paprika with ⅔ cup salad oil; ⅓ cup tarragon vinegar; 3 tablespoons lemon juice; and 2 teaspoons grated onion. Chill thoroughly.

CHUCK WAGON SALAD

For dressing, shake together ¼ cup salad oil; 2 tablespoons white wine vinegar; and 1 ounce blue cheese, crumbled (¼ cup), in screw-top jar. Chill thoroughly.

Rub bowl with cut end of 1 clove garlic. Add 4 cups torn lettuce; one 8½-ounce can (1 cup) limas, drained and chilled; 1 cup *each* sliced celery and sliced cucumber; and 2 medium tomatoes, cut in wedges. Season. Toss mixture with dressing. Serves 6.

WILTED SPINACH TOSS

A tang of orange penetrates throughout—

3 slices bacon
¼ cup vinegar
1 tablespoon salad oil
1½ teaspoons sugar
¼ teaspoon salt
⅛ teaspoon dried tarragon leaves, crushed
Dash freshly ground black pepper
. . .
¼ cup chopped celery
1 tablespoon sliced green onion
6 cups torn fresh spinach (about ½ pound)
2 medium oranges, peeled and cut in bite-size pieces

In large skillet, cook bacon till crisp; drain, reserving 2 tablespoons bacon drippings. Crumble bacon and set aside. Stir vinegar, oil, sugar, salt, tarragon, and pepper into reserved drippings; bring to boiling. Add chopped celery and sliced green onion.

Gradually add spinach, tossing just till leaves are coated and wilted slightly. Add oranges and crumbled bacon; toss lightly. Makes 6 to 8 servings.

ITALIAN ANCHOVY SALAD

1 2-ounce can anchovy fillets, drained
2 large tomatoes, peeled and cut in thin wedges
2 medium green peppers, cut in narrow strips
12 pitted ripe olives
8 green onions, chopped
. . .
¼ cup olive oil
2 tablespoons vinegar
Freshly ground black pepper
Shredded lettuce

Separate anchovy fillets into bowl; add tomatoes, green pepper, olives, and green onion. Combine oil and vinegar and drizzle over anchovy mixture. Sprinkle with pepper. Refrigerate about 1 hour. At serving time, spoon over shredded lettuce. Serves 4.

GREEN SALAD QUINTET

- ½ bunch watercress
- 6 romaine leaves
- 6 Boston lettuce leaves
- 4 escarole leaves
- 2 French endives

. . .

- 6 radishes, sliced
- 1 scallion, finely chopped
- 2 tablespoons olive oil
- 2 tablespoons wine vinegar
  Dash *each* garlic salt,
    monosodium glutamate,
    paprika, and freshly ground
    black pepper.

Rinse first 5 ingredients; drain. Tear leaves in bite-size pieces and slice endives. Combine greens with radishes and scallion. Combine remaining ingredients. Toss lightly with lettuce mixture. Makes 4 to 6 servings.

CURRY SALAD

- ½ teaspoon beef-flavored gravy
    base
- 1 cup mayonnaise or salad
    dressing
- 1 clove garlic, minced
- 1 tablespoon curry powder
- ¼ teaspoon Worcestershire sauce
- 6 to 8 drops bottled hot pepper
    sauce

. . .

- 6 cups torn mixed salad greens
- 4 cups torn fresh spinach
- 1 16-ounce can artichoke hearts,
    chilled, drained, and halved
- ¼ cup sliced radishes

For dressing, dissolve gravy base in ¼ cup hot water; blend into mayonnaise. Stir in garlic, curry, Worcestershire sauce, and hot pepper sauce. Chill. Combine remaining ingredients in large salad bowl. Toss lettuce mixture lightly with dressing. Serves 10.

"Spice of the East" dressing in Curry Salad flavors the meal with a nostalgia of India. Refrigerating the dressing several hours or overnight enhances the intriguing blend of ingredients.

TANGY SPINACH BOWL

Lemon and horseradish give it zip—

2 tablespoons sliced green onion
¼ cup butter or margarine
2 tablespoons all-purpose flour
¼ teaspoon salt
1 cup water
2 tablespoons lemon juice
1 tablespoon prepared horseradish
½ teaspoon Worcestershire sauce
2 hard-cooked eggs
1 pound fresh spinach, torn in bite-size pieces

In small saucepan, prepare dressing by cooking onion in butter about 1 minute; blend in flour and salt. Add water, lemon juice, horseradish, and Worcestershire sauce; cook and stir till mixture is boiling.

Dice 1 hard-cooked egg; add to dressing. Pour hot dressing over spinach in salad bowl; toss lightly. Slice remaining egg and arrange over salad. Sprinkle with paprika, if desired. Serve immediately. Serves 6 to 8.

FRUIT-VEGETABLE TOSS

An attractive salad for a special occasion—

12 cups torn lettuce
8 ounces sharp natural Cheddar cheese, cut in thin strips
½ cup sliced celery
⅔ cup salad oil
⅓ cup wine vinegar
½ cup sugar
1 tablespoon grated onion
1 teaspoon dry mustard
½ teaspoon salt
4 medium pared oranges, cut in bite-size pieces
2 medium nectarines, peeled and sliced

Combine lettuce, cheese, and celery in large salad bowl. To prepare dressing, beat together oil, vinegar, sugar, onion, dry mustard, and salt. Pour enough dressing over lettuce to coat lightly; toss. Top with orange pieces and nectarine slices. Toss again. Pass remaining dressing. Makes 12 servings.

FOO YUNG TOSS

A Chinese version of tossed salad—

1 head romaine, torn in bite-size pieces
1 16-ounce can bean sprouts, rinsed and drained
1 5-ounce can water chestnuts, drained and sliced
5 slices bacon, crisp-cooked and crumbled
2 hard-cooked eggs, sliced
1 cup salad oil
½ cup sugar
⅓ cup catsup
¼ cup vinegar
2 tablespoons grated onion
2 teaspoons Worcestershire sauce

In salad bowl, combine romaine, bean sprouts, water chestnuts, bacon, and eggs. Season to taste with salt and pepper. To prepare dressing, combine remaining ingredients in screw-top jar. Shake well. Pour over salad; toss lightly. Makes 6 to 8 servings.

CAMEMBERT SALAD

1 small head lettuce
4 ounces Camembert cheese, cubed
2 ounces sharp natural Cheddar cheese, shredded (½ cup)

Place 4 lettuce cups in salad bowl. Tear remaining lettuce into bite-size pieces (about 4 cups). Toss with cheeses and fill lettuce cups. Serve with a vinegar-oil or Italian salad dressing. Makes 4 servings.

SPINACH-AVOCADO BOWL

10 ounces fresh spinach, torn in bite-size pieces
2 medium avocados, peeled and sliced
½ pound bacon, crisp-cooked and crumbled
½ cup chopped peanuts

Place spinach in salad bowl. Arrange avocado slices, bacon, and nuts over. Serve with a Russian salad dressing. Serves 8 to 10.

TOSSING TIPS

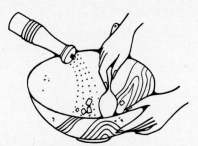

Try the Chef's flavor trick. Lightly sprinkle salt in a wooden salad bowl. Mash a clove of garlic into the salt with the back of a spoon. The fresh flavor of garlic will mingle pleasantly with that favorite tossed salad.

Roll-toss salads in a big bowl. Gently stroke downward to bottom with tool in one hand and up and over with tool in other hand. This down-and-over motion, with dressing delicately coating greens, assures the salad of superb taste.

Tear salad greens into bite-size pieces rather than cutting them with a knife. Tearing exposes the juicy insides and allows the dressing to become absorbed by the greens. Besides tasting fresher, torn greens make a more attractive looking tossed salad.

Hold the juicy tomato wedges till last when tossing a bowl of salad greens. This prevents the dressing from becoming diluted. For delicious crunch, add a few crisp croutons or coarsely chopped walnuts that have been browned with butter in a skillet over medium heat.

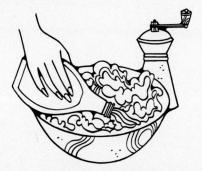

Always shake an oil-vinegar dressing before using. Shaking emulsifies the oil and vinegar and blends those carefully chosen herbs and spices. Add just enough dressing to the salad so every leaf glistens. Toss together lightly.

Salad tossing delayed? Don't let greens wilt. For short delays, keep them fresh under damp paper toweling wrung out of ice water. For longer delays, place bowl covered with damp paper toweling on a refrigerator shelf.

TOSSED SALAD COMBINATION GUIDE

Venture into the realm of leafy greens and vegetables with a flavorful salad creation that will give each menu spark and variety. To prepare the winning combinations given below, tear salad greens in bite-size pieces unless otherwise indicated. Add remaining ingredients *except* garnish and toss lightly with your favorite dressing. Garnish with the ingredient in the last column; serve immediately.

To Go Along With	Add These	Garnish With
Bibb lettuce	Tomato, cut in wedges	Hard-cooked egg, sliced
	Unpared cucumber, sliced	
	Avocado, peeled and sliced	
Boston lettuce	Hard-cooked egg, chopped	Parsley sprigs
	Fresh mushrooms, sliced	
	Chives, snipped	
Boston lettuce	Watercress	Parmesan cheese, grated
	Anchovy fillets	
Chinese cabbage	Leaf lettuce	Water chestnuts, sliced
	Celery, bias-cut	
	Radishes, sliced	
	Chives, snipped	
Curly endive	Iceberg lettuce	Hard-cooked egg, sliced
	Bacon, crisp-cooked and crumbled	
	Tomato, cut in wedges	
	Celery, sliced	
	Radishes, sliced	
	Green onion, chopped	
Iceberg lettuce	Carrot, shredded	Raisins
	Celery, diced	
	Mandarin oranges, well-drained	

To Go Along With	Add These	Garnish With
Iceberg lettuce	Raw cauliflowerets, thinly sliced	Blue cheese, crumbled
	Onion, sliced and separated into rings	
	Pimiento-stuffed green olives, sliced	
Leaf lettuce	Chicory	Walnut halves
	Watercress	
	Tomato, cut in wedges	
	Onion, thinly sliced	
	Cucumber, sliced	
Leaf lettuce	Curly endive	Cheddar cheese, cut in thin strips
	Tomato, finely diced	
	Green onion, sliced	
Leaf lettuce	Watercress	Almonds, toasted
	Raw spinach	
	Carrot curls	
	Pitted ripe olives, sliced	
Romaine	Tomato, diced	Artichoke hearts
	Green pepper, chopped	
	Romano cheese, grated	
Raw spinach	Bacon, crisp-cooked and crumbled	Canned French-fried onions
	Hard-cooked egg, chopped	
	Carrot, thinly sliced	
Raw spinach, shredded	Raw zucchini, sliced	Mushroom crowns
	Radishes, sliced	
	Green onion, sliced	

INVITING VEGETABLE MOLDS

CUCUMBER RING SUPREME

Cucumber-trim Layer
1 envelope (1 tablespoon) unflavored gelatin
2 tablespoons sugar
2 tablespoons lemon juice
1 8-ounce package cream cheese, cubed and softened
About 6 medium pared cucumbers
1 cup mayonnaise or salad dressing
3 tablespoons finely chopped onion
¼ cup snipped parsley

Prepare *Cucumber-trim Layer:* Mix ½ envelope (1½ teaspoons) unflavored gelatin, 1 tablespoon sugar, and ½ teaspoon salt in small saucepan. Add ¾ cup water; heat and stir till gelatin and sugar are dissolved. Stir in 2 tablespoons lemon juice. Pour into 6½-cup ring mold. Chill till partially set. Overlay thin slices from ½ unpared cucumber in bottom of mold. Chill till *almost* firm.

Meanwhile, mix the 1 envelope unflavored gelatin, sugar, and ¾ teaspoon salt in saucepan. Add ⅔ cup water; stir over low heat till gelatin and sugar are dissolved. Stir in lemon juice. Gradually beat hot gelatin mixture into softened cream cheese with rotary beater till mixture is smooth.

Halve cucumbers and scrape out seeds; grind using fine blade, or finely shred. Measure 2 cups drained ground cucumber and add with remaining ingredients to cream cheese mixture. Pour over almost firm gelatin in mold. Chill till firm. Makes 8 servings.

← **Cherry tomatoes and fresh watercress,** both perky and bright, are decorative additions to Cucumber Ring Supreme. Enjoy the creamy richness and cucumber crunch in every bite.

CARROT-CABBAGE MOLD

Pickle perfection salad laced with vegetables—

2 3-ounce packages lemon-flavored gelatin
¼ cup lemon juice
1 cup shredded cabbage
½ cup shredded carrots
½ cup diced celery
¼ cup diced sweet pickle *or* pickle relish

Dissolve gelatin in 2 cups boiling water; stir in 1½ cups cold water, lemon juice, and ¼ teaspoon salt. Chill till partially set. Fold in remaining ingredients. Pour into 5½-cup mold. Chill till firm. Makes 8 to 10 servings.

CABBAGE ASPIC

2 envelopes (2 tablespoons) unflavored gelatin
4 cups tomato juice
½ medium onion, sliced
3 branches celery, 3 inches long
2 lemon slices
2 bay leaves
Non-caloric liquid sweetener equal to 2 tablespoons sugar
2 teaspoons prepared horseradish
2 cups chopped cabbage *or* 1 cup chopped celery

Soften gelatin in ½ *cup* tomato juice; set aside. In saucepan, combine remaining tomato juice, onion, celery, lemon, and bay leaves. Bring to boiling; reduce heat and simmer, covered, for 10 minutes; strain. Add softened gelatin. Return to low heat and stir till gelatin is dissolved. Stir in non-caloric sweetener, horseradish, ½ teaspoon salt, and dash pepper. Chill till partially set. Fold in cabbage. Pour into eight ½-cup molds. Chill till firm. Makes 8 servings.

SPRING SALAD SOUFFLE

1 3-ounce package lime-flavored gelatin
1 10½-ounce can condensed cream of asparagus soup
½ cup mayonnaise or salad dressing
1 tablespoon vinegar
1 teaspoon grated onion
½ cup shredded unpared cucumber
¼ cup diced celery
1 tablespoon snipped parsley

In saucepan, mix gelatin and ½ cup water. Gradually blend in soup; heat and stir till gelatin is dissolved. Add next 3 ingredients and dash pepper to gelatin. Beat with rotary beater till mixture is smooth. Chill till gelatin mixture is partially set.

Pour gelatin into large chilled bowl; beat till thick and fluffy. Fold in remaining ingredients. Pour into 5½-cup ring mold; chill till firm. Makes 4 or 5 servings.

JELLIED POTATO SALAD

5 cups diced, peeled, cooked potatoes
1 tablespoon vinegar
1 cup chopped onion
1½ cups mayonnaise
1 tablespoon celery seed
2 3-ounce packages lemon-flavored gelatin
¼ cup vinegar
9 green pepper rings
9 red pepper rings *or* pimiento strips
1 cup diced cucumber

Sprinkle potatoes with the 1 tablespoon vinegar and 2 teaspoons salt. Toss with onion, mayonnaise, and celery seed; chill. Dissolve gelatin in 2½ cups boiling water; stir in the ¼ cup vinegar. To *half* the gelatin mixture add ¼ cup cold water. Pour into 9x 9x2-inch pan. Chill till partially set; arrange peppers atop gelatin. Chill till *almost* firm.

Meanwhile, chill remaining gelatin till partially set; beat till soft peaks form. Fold in potato mixture and cucumber. Spoon over gelatin in pan; chill till firm. Invert to unmold. Cut in squares. Makes 9 servings.

COLESLAW PARFAIT SALAD

Equally attractive made in individual molds—

1 3-ounce package lemon-flavored gelatin
½ cup mayonnaise or salad dressing
2 tablespoons vinegar
¼ teaspoon salt

. . .

1 cup finely shredded cabbage
½ cup diced celery
½ cup sliced radishes
2 tablespoons chopped green pepper
1 tablespoon chopped onion

Dissolve gelatin in 1 cup boiling water. Add ½ cup cold water, mayonnaise, vinegar, and salt; beat with rotary beater till smooth. Chill till partially set, then beat till light and fluffy. Fold in remaining ingredients. Pour into 3½-cup mold; chill till gelatin mixture is firm. Makes 5 or 6 servings.

EASY ASPIC

Dissolve two 3-ounce packages lemon-flavored gelatin in 1¾ cups boiling water. Stir in two 8-ounce cans (2 cups) tomato sauce, 2 tablespoons vinegar, ½ teaspoon salt, and ½ teaspoon seasoned salt. Pour into 4½-cup mold or eight ½-cup molds. Chill till firm. Makes 8 servings.

CREAMY BROCCOLI MOLD

Soften 1 envelope (1 tablespoon) unflavored gelatin in ¾ cup cold water. Cook one 10-ounce package frozen chopped broccoli following package directions, adding 2 chicken bouillon cubes, 1 tablespoon instant minced onion, and 1 teaspoon monosodium glutamate to cooking water. *Do not add salt. Do not drain.* Add softened gelatin and stir till gelatin is dissolved. Cool. Stir ½ cup dairy sour cream into broccoli mixture.

Fold in ½ cup chopped celery, ¼ cup chopped canned pimiento, 2 tablespoons snipped parsley, and 2 tablespoons lemon juice. Pour gelatin mixture into 5½-cup ring mold; chill till firm. Makes 6 to 8 servings.

VEGETABLE CREAM MOLDS

Dissolve one 3-ounce package lemon-flavored gelatin and 2 beef bouillon cubes in 1 cup boiling water; chill till partially set. Add 1 cup dairy sour cream and 2 tablespoons tarragon vinegar; beat with rotary beater till smooth. Fold in ½ cup *each* chopped celery, chopped radishes, and chopped unpared cucumber, and 2 tablespoons *each* chopped green pepper and chopped green onion. Pour into six ½-cup molds; chill till firm. Makes 6 servings.

BEET-PINEAPPLE MOLD

> 1 16-ounce can shoestring beets
> 1 8¾-ounce can crushed pineapple
> 2 3-ounce packages lemon-flavored gelatin
> 2 cups boiling water
> 2 tablespoons lemon juice
> Dash salt

Drain beets and pineapple, reserving 1½ cups of the combined liquids. Dissolve gelatin in boiling water; stir in reserved liquid, lemon juice, and salt. Chill till partially set, then fold in drained beets and pineapple. Pour gelatin mixture into 6½-cup mold or eight to ten ½-cup molds. Chill till gelatin mixture is firm. Makes 8 to 10 servings.

VEGETABLE LIME RING

> 1 3-ounce package lime-flavored gelatin
> ¾ cup boiling water
>   •   •   •
> ¾ cup shredded unpared cucumber
> ¼ cup finely sliced green onion
> 1 8-ounce carton (1 cup) cream-style cottage cheese
> 1 cup mayonnaise or salad dressing
> 1 teaspoon prepared horseradish
> ¼ teaspoon salt

Dissolve gelatin in boiling water; chill till partially set. Combine remaining ingredients and fold into gelatin. Pour gelatin mixture into 3½-cup ring mold. Chill till gelatin mixture is firm. Makes 5 or 6 servings.

PERFECTION SALAD

An all-time favorite—

> 2 envelopes (2 tablespoons) unflavored gelatin
> ½ cup sugar
> 1 teaspoon salt
> 1½ cups boiling water
> 1½ cups cold water
> ⅓ cup white vinegar
> 2 tablespoons lemon juice
> 2 cups finely shredded cabbage
> 1 cup chopped celery
> ½ cup chopped green pepper
> ¼ cup chopped canned pimiento

Mix gelatin, sugar, and salt. Add boiling water and stir till gelatin, sugar, and salt are dissolved. Stir in cold water, vinegar, and lemon juice; chill till partially set. Fold cabbage, celery, green pepper, and pimiento into gelatin. Pour gelatin mixture into 5½-cup ring mold. Chill till firm. Serves 8 to 10.

CUCUMBER-CABBAGE MOLD

The center of the ring is an ideal spot for a small bowl of mayonnaise—

> 2 3-ounce packages lime-flavored gelatin
> 2 cups boiling water
> 1¾ cups cold water
> 2 tablespoons vinegar
> 1 teaspoon prepared horseradish
> ½ teaspoon salt
>   •   •   •
> 1 large unpared cucumber
> 1 cup chopped cabbage

Dissolve gelatin in boiling water. Stir cold water, vinegar, horseradish, and salt into dissolved gelatin. Chill till partially set. Pour ½ *cup* of the gelatin mixture into 5½-cup ring mold. Cut 10 to 15 paper-thin slices of unpared cucumber and arrange on gelatin in mold. Chill till *almost* firm.

Dice enough unpared cucumber to make 1 cup; fold cucumber and chopped cabbage into remaining partially set gelatin. Carefully pour cabbage mixture over almost firm gelatin layer. Chill till firm. Pass mayonnaise, if desired. Makes 8 to 10 servings.

Make-ahead salads like Calico Vegetable Molds ease last minute dinner duties. Premolded individual servings need only be placed on lettuce-lined plates and topped with a dollop of dressing.

CALICO VEGETABLE MOLDS

- 1 3-ounce package lemon-flavored gelatin
- 2 tablespoons vinegar
- 1 8-ounce can peas and carrots, drained
- ¼ cup sliced radishes
- 2 tablespoons sliced green onion

Dissolve gelatin in 1 cup boiling water; stir in ¾ cup cold water, vinegar, and ¼ teaspoon salt. Chill till partially set. Fold in peas and carrots, radishes, and green onion. Pour into six ½-cup molds. Chill till firm. Pass mayonnaise, if desired. Makes 6 servings.

"ONE CUP" COTTAGE RING

Dissolve one 3-ounce package lime-flavored gelatin in 1 cup boiling water. Add 1 cup mayonnaise or salad dressing and beat with rotary beater till smooth. Chill till partially set. Fold in one 8-ounce carton (1 cup) large curd cream-style cottage cheese, 1 cup chopped celery, and 1 cup diced green pepper. Pour into 4½-cup mold. Chill till firm. Makes 6 servings.

TOMATO ASPIC SOUFFLE

- 1 6-ounce can (⅔ cup) evaporated milk
- 3 cups tomato juice
- 2 bay leaves
- 4 black peppercorns
- ½ teaspoon onion salt
- ¼ teaspoon celery salt
- ¼ teaspoon dried oregano leaves, crushed
- 2 envelopes (2 tablespoons) unflavored gelatin
- 2 3-ounce packages cream cheese, softened

Pour milk into freezer tray. Freeze till soft ice crystals form around edges. In saucepan, blend *2 cups* of the tomato juice with the next 5 ingredients. Simmer, covered, for 5 minutes; strain. Soften gelatin in ½ *cup* cold tomato juice; stir into hot mixture till gelatin is dissolved. Cool. With rotary beater, gradually beat remaining juice into cream cheese; stir into gelatin mixture.

Chill till partially set. Whip icy cold evaporated milk till stiff peaks form; fold into gelatin mixture. Pour into 6½-cup mold; chill till firm. Makes 10 to 12 servings.

MOLDED ASPARAGUS SALAD

- 1 envelope (1 tablespoon) unflavored gelatin
- 1 10½-ounce can condensed cream of asparagus soup
- 1 tablespoon lemon juice
- ¼ teaspoon salt
- 1 8-ounce carton (1 cup) cream-style cottage cheese
- ½ cup dairy sour cream
- 1 10½-ounce can asparagus spears, drained and cut
- ½ cup chopped celery
- 2 tablespoons chopped canned pimiento

In saucepan, soften gelatin in ¼ cup cold water. Stir over low heat till gelatin is dissolved. Blend soup, lemon juice, and salt into gelatin; beat in cottage cheese and sour cream. Chill gelatin mixture till partially set, then fold in remaining ingredients. Pour into 4½-cup mold. Chill till firm. Serves 5 or 6.

PIMIENTO CHEESE MOLD

    1 3-ounce package lemon-flavored
       gelatin
    ½ teaspoon salt
    1 cup boiling water
    1 5-ounce jar process cheese
       spread with pimiento
    ¼ cup mayonnaise or salad
       dressing
    ¼ cup cold water
    2 to 3 teaspoons vinegar
       Dash bottled hot pepper sauce
        • • •
    ½ cup chopped celery
    2 tablespoons finely chopped
       onion
    2 tablespoons finely chopped
       green pepper

Dissolve gelatin and salt in boiling water. Add cheese spread and mayonnaise; beat with rotary beater till smooth. Stir in cold water, vinegar, and hot pepper sauce. Chill gelatin mixture till partially set.

Fold remaining ingredients into gelatin mixture. Pour into 3½-cup mold. Chill salad till firm. Makes 4 servings.

BLENDER CUCUMBER SALAD

An appliance does all the work—

    1 large cucumber, pared
    1 3-ounce package lemon-flavored
       gelatin
    Cottage Cheese Dressing

Slice cucumber into blender container. Cover and blend on high speed till pureed. Stop blender as needed to push cucumber down from sides. Measure cucumber; add water, if necessary, to make 1 cup.

Dissolve gelatin in 1¼ cups boiling water; stir in cucumber. Chill gelatin mixture till partially set, stirring occasionally. Pour into 3½-cup ring mold. Chill till firm. Serve with Cottage Cheese Dressing. Serves 4 to 6.

Cottage Cheese Dressing: In blender container, combine one 8-ounce carton (1 cup) cream-style cottage cheese; 2 tablespoons sugar; and 4 teaspoons lemon juice. Blend till creamy. Add 2 tablespoons milk, one at a time, till desired consistency.

BARBECUE BEAN MOLD

A splendid backyard barbecue salad—

Soften 2 envelopes (2 tablespoons) unflavored gelatin in ½ cup tomato juice. Add 2 tablespoons brown sugar and 1 teaspoon prepared mustard; stir over low heat till gelatin and sugar are dissolved. Stir in 1 cup tomato juice and 2 tablespoons lemon juice. Chill till partially set.

Fold one 16-ounce can barbecue beans, ½ cup chopped celery, and 1 tablespoon finely chopped onion into gelatin mixture. Pour into 4½-cup mold. Chill till firm. Unmold on lettuce-lined platter. Makes 8 servings.

CONFETTI RELISH MOLD

Dissolve one 3-ounce package lemon-flavored gelatin and 2 beef bouillon cubes in 1 cup boiling water; stir in 1 tablespoon tarragon vinegar. Chill till partially set. Add 1 cup dairy sour cream to gelatin; beat with rotary beater till smooth. Fold in ½ cup chopped unpared cucumber, ¼ cup sliced radishes, ¼ cup finely chopped green pepper, and 2 tablespoons sliced green onion. Pour into 3½-cup mold. Chill till firm. Serves 6.

CREAMY RICE MOLD

    2 envelopes (2 tablespoons)
       unflavored gelatin
    2 13¾-ounce cans (3½ cups)
       chicken broth
    ¾ cup mayonnaise or salad
       dressing
    2 tablespoons lemon juice
        • • •
    1 cup whipping cream, whipped
    2½ cups cooked rice
    ¾ cup chopped celery
    ¼ cup sliced green onion

Soften gelatin in ½ cup cold water. Heat broth to boiling. Add softened gelatin and stir till dissolved. Add mayonnaise and lemon juice; beat with rotary beater till smooth. Chill mixture till partially set, then whip till light and fluffy. Fold in remaining ingredients. Pour into 8½-cup ring mold. Chill till firm. Makes 10 to 12 servings.

Make Tomato-celery Aspic the keynote for a summer patio supper. Pile spicy Swedish Pickled Shrimp or a favorite seafood or chicken salad in the center of the celery-dotted tomato ring. Trim plate with curly endive. The peppy shrimp can also double as appetizers or make a salad in themselves.

TOMATO-CELERY ASPIC

Soften 2 envelopes (2 tablespoons) unflavored gelatin in 1 cup cold tomato juice. In saucepan, mix 2 cups tomato juice with 1/3 cup chopped onion, 1/4 cup snipped celery leaves, 2 tablespoons brown sugar, 1 teaspoon salt, 2 small bay leaves, and 4 whole cloves. Simmer, uncovered, 5 minutes. Strain to remove vegetables and seasonings.

Dissolve softened gelatin in seasoned hot tomato mixture. Add 1 cup tomato juice and 3 tablespoons lemon juice. Chill till gelatin mixture is partially set.

Fold in 1 cup chopped celery. Pour into 5 1/2-cup ring mold. Chill till firm. Unmold and fill center of ring with Swedish Pickled Shrimp. Makes 8 to 10 servings.

SWEDISH PICKLED SHRIMP

In saucepan, cover 1 1/2 pounds frozen shrimp in shells with boiling water. Add 4 celery tops, 2 tablespoons mixed pickling spices, and 1 1/2 teaspoons salt. Cover and simmer 5 minutes. Drain, peel, and clean shrimp under cold water. Combine shrimp with 1 cup sliced onion, separated into rings; 4 bay leaves; and Pickling Marinade in shallow dish. Cover; chill at least 24 hours, spooning marinade over shrimp occasionally. Drain shrimp; spoon into center of aspic.

Pickling Marinade: Blend together 1 1/2 cups salad oil, 3/4 cup white vinegar, 3 tablespoons capers with liquid, 2 teaspoons celery seed, 1 1/2 teaspoons salt, and few drops bottled hot pepper sauce. Pour over shrimp.

ASPARAGUS MOLD

> 2 tablespoons (2 envelopes)
>   unflavored gelatin
> ½ cup sugar
> ¼ teaspoon salt
> 3½ cups cold water
> ⅓ cup white vinegar
> 3 tablespoons lemon juice
> 1 teaspoon grated onion
> 1 cup finely chopped celery
> ⅓ cup chopped canned
>   pimiento
> 1 14½-ounce can asparagus cuts,
>   drained
>   Mayonnaise or salad dressing

In saucepan, combine gelatin, sugar, and salt. Add 1½ *cups* of the cold water and vinegar; stir over low heat till gelatin and sugar are dissolved. Add lemon juice, onion, and remaining water. Chill till partially set.

Fold in celery and pimiento. Arrange *one-third* of the asparagus in bottom of 6½-cup mold. Carefully pour in *one-third* of the gelatin mixture. Repeat layers, ending with gelatin. Chill till firm. Serve with mayonnaise or salad dressing. Makes 10 to 12 servings.

POTATO SALAD MOLD

> 1 envelope (1 tablespoon)
>   unflavored gelatin
> 2 tablespoons sugar
> ¼ cup lemon juice
> 4 cups diced, peeled, cooked
>   potatoes
> ¾ cup chopped celery
> 3 hard-cooked eggs, chopped
> ¼ cup sliced pimiento-stuffed
>   green olives
> ¼ cup chopped green pepper
> ¼ cup snipped parsley
> 1 cup mayonnaise
> ½ cup whipping cream, whipped

Mix gelatin, sugar, and ¾ teaspoon salt in saucepan. Add 1¼ cups water; stir over low heat till gelatin and sugar are dissolved. Add lemon juice. Cool to room temperature. Stir next 6 ingredients into gelatin mixture. Fold in mayonnaise and whipped cream. Spoon into 7½-cup mold or 9x9x2-inch pan. Chill till firm. Makes 8 or 9 servings.

RICE AND CARROT MOLD

> 1 3-ounce package lime-flavored
>   gelatin
> ¼ teaspoon salt
> 1 cup boiling water
> 1 8¾-ounce can crushed
>   pineapple
> ⅓ cup mayonnaise
> 1 cup cooked rice
> ½ cup grated carrot
> ¼ cup toasted slivered almonds

Dissolve gelatin and salt in boiling water. Drain pineapple, reserving syrup. Add enough water to syrup to make 1 cup; stir into gelatin. Chill till partially set. Add mayonnaise and beat with rotary beater till smooth. Fold in pineapple, rice, carrot, and nuts. Pour into 4½-cup mold. Chill till firm. Makes 5 or 6 servings.

CRAN-PERFECTION SALADS

> 1 envelope (1 tablespoon)
>   unflavored gelatin
> 1 16-ounce can jellied cranberry
>   sauce
> 1 cup shredded cabbage
> ½ cup diced celery
> 1 tablespoon vinegar

Soften gelatin in ½ cup cold water. Add ¼ teaspoon salt and stir over low heat till gelatin is dissolved. Beat cranberry sauce till smooth. Stir in gelatin mixture, cabbage, celery, and vinegar. Spoon into six ½-cup molds. Chill till firm. Makes 6 servings.

SPRINGTIME CALICO MOLD

> 1 4-serving envelope low-calorie
>   lime-flavored gelatin
> 3 tablespoons lemon juice
> ½ cup shredded cucumber
> ¼ cup thinly sliced radishes
> ½ cup cubed Cheddar cheese

LOW CALORIE · LOW CALORIE

Dissolve gelatin in 1 cup boiling water. Stir in ¼ teaspoon salt, ¾ cup cold water, and lemon juice. Chill till partially set. Fold in cucumber, radishes, and cheese. Pour into 3½-cup mold. Chill till firm. Serves 6.

FROM CABBAGE TO COLESLAW

BEAN AND BACON SLAW

In skillet, fry 4 slices bacon till crisp. Drain bacon, reserving drippings; crumble and set aside. Cook ¼ cup chopped onion in reserved drippings in skillet till lightly browned. Stir in ⅓ cup wine vinegar, 1 teaspoon sugar, ½ teaspoon salt, and dash pepper; simmer several minutes. Pour over mixture of 2 cups shredded cabbage; one 17-ounce can baby limas, drained; and one 3-ounce can sliced mushrooms, drained. Toss. Sprinkle with bacon. Makes 6 servings.

COTTAGE CHEESE SLAW

Blend together ½ cup cream-style cottage cheese, ½ cup mayonnaise or salad dressing, 2 tablespoons vinegar, ½ teaspoon caraway seed, ½ teaspoon onion juice, and ¼ teaspoon Worcestershire sauce. (If stronger caraway flavor is desired, chill mayonnaise mixture several hours.) Just before serving, toss mayonnaise mixture lightly with 8 cups shredded cabbage, chilled. Serves 8 to 10.

COLESLAW VINAIGRETTE

    2 cups shredded cabbage
    ⅓ cup sliced green onion
    ¼ cup snipped parsley
    2 tablespoons sugar
    3 tablespoons vinegar
    2 tablespoons salad oil
    1 hard-cooked egg, chilled

Combine cabbage, onion, and parsley; chill. Blend together next 3 ingredients and 1 teaspoon salt, stirring till sugar is dissolved; chill. Pour vinegar mixture over vegetable mixture; toss lightly. Separate yolk from white of hard-cooked egg. Cut white into thin wedges. Arrange atop salad. Sieve yolk over. Makes 6 servings.

CHINESE CABBAGE TOSS

Delicately-flavored Oriental coleslaw—

    4 cups shredded Chinese cabbage
    1 3-ounce can sliced mushrooms, drained
    1 tablespoon chopped onion
    ½ cup mayonnaise
    1 tablespoon soy sauce
    ½ cup chow mein noodles

Combine cabbage, mushrooms, and onion. Blend together mayonnaise and soy; toss lightly with cabbage mixture. Just before serving, top with noodles. Serves 6 to 8.

TOMATO COLESLAW

Combine 2 cups shredded cabbage; 18 cherry tomatoes, halved; ¼ cup diced cucumber; and 2 teaspoons minced onion. Chill. Blend together ¼ cup mayonnaise or salad dressing, 2 tablespoons French salad dressing, 1½ teaspoons lemon juice, 1 teaspoon sugar, ½ teaspoon salt, and dash pepper; chill. Just before serving, toss mayonnaise mixture lightly with cabbage mixture. Makes 6 to 8 servings.

APPLE-PINEAPPLE SLAW

    3 cups shredded cabbage
    1 8¾-ounce can pineapple tidbits, drained (⅔ cup)
    1 cup diced unpared apple
    ½ cup chopped celery
    ½ cup mayonnaise
    1 cup miniature marshmallows

Combine all ingredients *except* marshmallows; toss lightly. Chill. Just before serving, fold in marshmallows. Trim with apple slices, if desired. Makes 10 to 12 servings.

Spark the meal in the American tradition with a bowl full of coleslaw. In Creamy Cabbage Slaw, a celery seed dressing lightly coats crisp shreds of cabbage and green onion rings. On another day, use all red or a combination of red and green cabbage for a pleasant change.

CREAMY CABBAGE SLAW

    6 cups shredded cabbage
  ¼ cup sliced green onion
        . . .
    1 cup mayonnaise or salad
       dressing
    2 tablespoons sugar
    2 tablespoons vinegar
    2 teaspoons celery seed
    1 teaspoon salt

Combine shredded cabbage and sliced green onion; chill. Blend together mayonnaise or salad dressing, sugar, vinegar, celery seed, and salt, stirring till sugar is dissolved; chill. Toss mayonnaise mixture lightly with cabbage mixture. Makes 10 servings.

SPRING GARDEN TOSS

    4 cups shredded cabbage
  ½ cup chopped celery
  ¼ cup chopped green pepper
  ¼ cup shredded carrot
  ¼ cup sliced radishes
    1 tablespoon chopped onion
  ½ cup dairy sour cream
    2 tablespoons tarragon vinegar
    1 tablespoon sugar
  ½ teaspoon salt

Combine cabbage, celery, green pepper, carrot, radishes, and onion; chill. Combine remaining ingredients; chill. Just before serving, toss sour cream mixture lightly with vegetable mixture. Makes 8 servings.

POLYNESIAN COLESLAW

2 cups shredded lettuce
2 cups shredded cabbage
½ cup chopped unpared cucumber
2 tablespoons milk
¼ cup flaked coconut
⅔ cup mayonnaise or salad
   dressing
¼ teaspoon salt
   Dash pepper

Combine lettuce, cabbage, and cucumber; chill. Pour milk over coconut; let stand 10 minutes. To prepare dressing, blend together mayonnaise, salt, and pepper; stir in coconut mixture. Toss dressing lightly with cabbage mixture. Makes 5 or 6 servings.

BACON CURRY COLESLAW

½ cup mayonnaise or salad
   dressing
2 tablespoons vinegar
1 teaspoon sugar
¼ teaspoon salt
¼ teaspoon curry powder
6 cups shredded cabbage, chilled
5 to 6 slices bacon, crisp-cooked
   and crumbled

Combine mayonnaise, vinegar, sugar, salt, curry powder, and dash freshly ground black pepper. Chill. Combine cabbage and bacon. Toss dressing lightly with cabbage mixture. Serves 12 to 14.

PEANUTTY COLESLAW

½ cup mayonnaise or salad
   dressing
¼ cup dairy sour cream
2 tablespoons sugar
2 tablespoons vinegar
¼ teaspoon monosodium glutamate
6 cups shredded cabbage, chilled
½ cup salted peanuts

To prepare dressing, blend together mayonnaise, sour cream, sugar, vinegar, and monosodium glutamate. Add to shredded cabbage and toss lightly. Mix in peanuts. Serve immediately. Makes 6 servings.

A sharp knife cuts even shreds of cabbage for coleslaw. Quarter the head; hold firmly to slice.

For fine, juicy slaw, shred cabbage with knife, then chop finely with a three-edged chopper.

A shredder makes fine, short shreds. Hold on board or over bowl; push quarter heads across.

BLUE CHEESE SLAW

  6 cups shredded cabbage
  2 tablespoons chopped canned
      pimiento
  2 tablespoons chopped green onion
      tops

    . . .

  ½ cup dairy sour cream
  2 tablespoons mayonnaise or
      salad dressing
  1 tablespoon lemon juice
  ½ teaspoon sugar
  4 ounces blue cheese,
      crumbled (1 cup)
  2 hard-cooked eggs, sliced

Combine first 3 ingredients; chill. To prepare dressing, blend together sour cream, dash salt, and remaining ingredients *except* eggs. Toss dressing lightly with cabbage mixture. Garnish with egg slices. Serves 10 to 12.

CABBAGE CUCUMBER SLAW

  3 cups shredded cabbage
  1 cup shredded red cabbage
  1 cup halved slices unpared
      cucumber
  ½ cup chopped celery
  2 tablespoons chopped onion
  2 tablespoons French salad
      dressing
  2 tablespoons mayonnaise or
      salad dressing

Combine first 5 ingredients; chill. Season to taste with salt and pepper. At serving time, blend French salad dressing and mayonnaise; toss with cabbage mixture. Serves 8.

CABBAGE BOWLS

Loosen outer green leaves of large head of cabbage but *do not* break off. Cut remainder of head in 8 sections *halfway* down. Hollow out center, leaving shell of 6 to 8 leaves. Place upside down in ice water to crisp. Drain. Shred center for slaw; refill bowl.

Or, make bowl by loosening outer leaves; spread out petal fashion. Hollow out center to within 1 inch of sides and bottom. Shred center for slaw. Refill bowl with slaw.

KIDNEY BEAN COLESLAW

  3 cups shredded cabbage
  1 8-ounce can kidney beans,
      chilled and drained
  ¼ cup sweet pickle relish
  ¼ cup thinly sliced green onion

    . . .

  ¼ cup mayonnaise or salad
      dressing
  3 tablespoons chili sauce
  ¼ teaspoon celery seed
      Dash salt

Combine shredded cabbage, kidney beans, sweet pickle relish, and green onion; chill. To prepare dressing, blend together mayonnaise, chili sauce, celery seed, and salt; toss with cabbage mixture. Makes 10 servings.

BEET AND CABBAGE SLAW

  ½ 16-ounce jar pickled beets
  4 cups shredded cabbage
  2 tablespoons chopped green
      pepper
  ½ cup mayonnaise or salad
      dressing

Drain pickled beets, reserving 1½ tablespoons liquid; chop drained beets. Combine beets, shredded cabbage, and chopped green pepper; chill. At serving time, prepare dressing by blending mayonnaise and reserved beet liquid; toss dressing lightly with cabbage mixture. Makes 8 servings.

SESAME SLAW

LOW CALORIE · LOW CALORIE ·

  2 cups shredded cabbage
  ¼ cup chopped green pepper
  2 tablespoons chopped onion
  3 tablespoons vinegar
      Non-caloric liquid sweetener
      equal to 8 teaspoons sugar
  ½ teaspoon salt
  ½ teaspoon toasted sesame seed

Combine shredded cabbage, chopped green pepper, and chopped onion; chill. Combine vinegar, non-caloric sweetener, salt, and toasted sesame seed; toss lightly with cabbage mixture. Makes 8 servings.

YEAR 'ROUND POTATO AND MACARONI SALADS

GERMAN MACARONI SALAD

Pasta tossed in a hot dressing—

  1 3-ounce can sliced mushrooms
  5 slices bacon
  ½ cup sugar
  3 tablespoons all-purpose flour
  ⅓ cup vinegar

. . .

  ½ 7-ounce package uncooked elbow
    macaroni
  ½ cup chopped green onion
  ½ cup chopped celery

Drain mushrooms, reserving liquid; add enough water to reserved liquid to make 1 cup. In 3-quart saucepan, fry bacon till crisp; drain, reserving drippings. Crumble bacon; set aside. Combine sugar, flour, ½ teaspoon salt, and ⅛ teaspoon pepper; blend into reserved drippings in saucepan. Combine vinegar and reserved 1 cup liquid. Add to flour mixture; cook and stir till thickened and bubbly.

Meanwhile, cook macaroni following package directions; drain. In saucepan, lightly toss macaroni with dressing, mushrooms, bacon, onion, and celery. Spoon into serving dish. Garnish with radishes and parsley, if desired. Serve immediately. Serves 8 to 10.

HOT DILL POTATO SALAD

In saucepan, melt 1 tablespoon butter or margarine over low heat. Stir in 1 tablespoon all-purpose flour, 1 teaspoon salt, ¼ teaspoon dried dillweed, and ⅛ teaspoon pepper. Add 1 cup milk all at once; cook and stir till thickened and bubbly. Blend in ½ cup mayonnaise or salad dressing and 2 tablespoons finely chopped onion; fold in 4 cups diced, peeled, cooked potatoes. Spoon into serving dish; sprinkle with paprika. Serve immediately. Serves 4 to 6.

SWEET POTATO SALAD

Featuring fall foods—

Combine 2 cups cooked sweet potatoes cut in chunks; 1 medium apple, diced; ½ cup diced celery; ½ cup chopped walnuts; ¼ cup chopped dates; and ½ teaspoon salt. Blend together ¼ cup dairy sour cream, ¼ cup mayonnaise or salad dressing, and 2 tablespoons milk. Fold sour cream mixture into potato mixture. Chill. Serve potato salad on lettuce-lined plates. Serves 8.

CALICO POTATO SALAD

  6 cups diced cooked potatoes
  ½ cup diced cucumber
  ½ cup chopped onion
  ¼ cup chopped green pepper
  3 tablespoons chopped canned
    pimiento
  1½ teaspoons salt
  ¾ teaspoon celery seed
  ¼ teaspoon pepper
  2 hard-cooked eggs
  ½ cup whipping cream, whipped
  ½ cup mayonnaise
  2 tablespoons vinegar
  1 tablespoon prepared mustard

Combine first 8 ingredients. Coarsely chop eggs, reserving 1 whole egg yolk. Add chopped eggs to potato mixture. Chill. Combine remaining ingredients, *except* yolk; toss with potato mixture ½ hour before serving. To serve, spoon into lettuce-lined bowl. Sieve reserved yolk over. Serves 10 to 12.

Calico Potato Salad describes this tangy-dressed →
salad dotted with green pepper and pimiento. Serve it with roll-ups made by rolling green onions with tops in slices of ham and cheese.

PATIO POTATO SALAD

An ideal outdoor barbecue dish—

⅓ cup sugar
1 tablespoon cornstarch
½ cup milk
¼ cup vinegar
1 egg
4 tablespoons butter or margarine
¾ teaspoon celery seed
¼ teaspoon dry mustard
¼ cup chopped onion
¼ cup mayonnaise or salad dressing
7 medium potatoes, cooked, peeled, and diced
3 hard-cooked eggs, chopped
Paprika

In saucepan, combine sugar and cornstarch; add next 6 ingredients and ¾ teaspoon salt. Cook and stir over low heat till bubbly. Remove from heat; add onion and mayonnaise. Cool. Combine potatoes and hard-cooked eggs; gently fold in dressing. Chill. Just before serving, sprinkle with paprika. Serves 6.

PARSLEYED POTATO SALAD

Molding in a loaf dish adds interest—

4 cups diced, peeled, cooked potatoes
¼ cup sliced celery
3 tablespoons snipped parsley
2 tablespoons chopped green pepper
2 tablespoons chopped green onion
2 tablespoons chopped dill pickle
¾ cup mayonnaise or salad dressing
2 tablespoons clear French salad dressing with herbs and spices
¾ teaspoon seasoned salt
¼ teaspoon dry mustard

Combine first 6 ingredients; toss lightly. Blend together remaining ingredients and dash pepper; gently fold into potato mixture. Pack into 8½x4½x2½-inch loaf dish; chill. Unmold on lettuce-lined plate; trim with additional parsley, if desired. Serves 4 or 5.

CAROUSEL SALAD

½ 7-ounce package spaghetti, broken, cooked, drained, and cooled (about 2 cups)
1 cup shredded carrots
½ cup diced celery
½ cup mayonnaise or salad dressing
2 tablespoons chopped dill pickle
1 teaspoon dill pickle juice
¼ teaspoon dried basil leaves, crushed

Combine cooked spaghetti, carrots, and celery. Blend together remaining ingredients and ½ teaspoon salt. Toss with spaghetti mixture. Chill. Makes 6 to 8 servings.

CHEDDAR POTATO SALAD

To 8 warm medium potatoes, cooked, peeled, and cubed, add 2 tablespoons snipped parsley, 2 tablespoons salad oil, 1 tablespoon grated onion, 1 teaspoon salt, and ¼ teaspoon pepper. Combine 1 cup chicken broth and 1 tablespoon white wine vinegar. Pour over potato mixture; toss lightly.

Chill mixture 1 hour, stirring occasionally. Before serving, fold in 1 cup shredded natural Cheddar cheese. Makes 8 servings.

BLUE CHEESE-SPUD SALAD

5 cups cubed, peeled, cooked potatoes
1 cup chopped celery
4 hard-cooked eggs, chopped
½ cup sliced green onion
¼ cup chopped green pepper
1 cup dairy sour cream
⅓ cup evaporated milk
1 ounce blue cheese, crumbled (¼ cup)
2 tablespoons vinegar
¼ teaspoon dry mustard
⅛ teaspoon pepper

Sprinkle cooked potatoes with 1 teaspoon salt. Combine potatoes, celery, eggs, onion, and green pepper. Blend together remaining ingredients. Pour over potato mixture; toss lightly. Chill. Makes 10 to 12 servings.

COUNTRY POTATO SALAD

New potatoes and lettuce pair up—

  1 pound (8 to 10) small new
      potatoes, cooked and peeled
  3 cups torn lettuce
  2 hard-cooked eggs, diced
  3 tablespoons thinly sliced green
      onion
  6 slices bacon
  ¼ cup vinegar
  1 teaspoon seasoned salt
  ¼ teaspoon celery seed
  ⅛ teaspoon pepper

Leave very small potatoes whole; halve or quarter larger ones. In bowl, combine potatoes, lettuce, eggs, and onion. In skillet, cook bacon till crisp; drain, reserving ¼ cup drippings. Crumble bacon; add to salad.

To reserved drippings in skillet, add vinegar, seasoned salt, celery seed, and pepper. Heat mixture to boiling then pour over potato mixture. Toss quickly; serve immediately. Makes 4 to 6 servings.

GINGERY MACARONI SALAD

Salad suitable for a "Sultan"—

  ½ 7-ounce package elbow
      macaroni, cooked and drained
      (about 2 cups)
  ¼ cup golden raisins
  ¼ cup chopped celery
      • • •
  ½ cup mayonnaise or salad
      dressing
  1 tablespoon chopped onion
  1 teaspoon chopped candied ginger
  ¼ teaspoon salt
  ¼ teaspoon curry powder
      Dash garlic salt
      Dash pepper
  2 tablespoons coarsely chopped
      peanuts

Combine macaroni, raisins, and celery. Blend together mayonnaise, onion, candied ginger, salt, curry, garlic salt, and pepper. Toss mayonnaise mixture lightly with macaroni mixture. Chill. Serve in lettuce cups; garnish with peanuts. Makes 4 to 6 servings.

SKILLET POTATO SALAD

An easy version of old-fashioned German potato salad makes a hit when served with a cheese and sausage assortment—

  6 medium potatoes, cooked,
      peeled, and diced
  8 slices bacon
  ½ cup chopped onion
  1 10½-ounce can condensed cream
      of celery soup
  ⅓ cup milk
  2 tablespoons sweet pickle relish
  2 tablespoons vinegar
  ½ teaspoon salt
      • • •
      Parsley sprigs
  1 hard-cooked egg, cut in wedges

Keep potatoes warm. In large skillet, cook bacon till crisp; drain, reserving ¼ cup drippings. Crumble bacon and set aside. Add chopped onion to drippings in skillet and cook just till tender. Blend in condensed soup, milk, pickle relish, vinegar, and salt. Heat to boiling, stirring constantly.

Gently stir in warm diced potatoes and crumbled bacon, reserving 1 tablespoon bacon for topping. Heat through. Sprinkle remaining bacon over top of potato salad; garnish with sprigs of parsley and hard-cooked egg wedges. Makes 4 to 6 servings.

For a casual supper, prepare and serve garnished Skillet Potato Salad in an electric skillet.

Look what's in a new dress. An old-time pasta favorite is now Macaroni-cheese Salad. Celery and carrot add color and crunch to shell macaroni.

Serve this hearty flavorful salad often—perfect for brunch, a satisfying main dish for supper, and a favorite to round out the barbecue picnic.

MACARONI-CHEESE SALAD

6 ounces uncooked shell macaroni
(about 1½ cups)
1 cup sliced celery
1 cup shredded carrots
¼ cup chopped onion
1 10¾-ounce can condensed
Cheddar cheese soup
¼ cup salad oil
2 tablespoons vinegar
1 teaspoon sugar
1 teaspoon prepared mustard
1 teaspoon Worcestershire sauce

Cook macaroni following package directions; drain and cool. Combine macaroni, celery, carrots, and onion. In small bowl, beat together soup, remaining ingredients, ½ teaspoon salt, and dash pepper. Spoon atop macaroni mixture; toss. Chill. Serves 4 to 6.

POTATO-APPLE SALAD

Combine 4 cups cubed, peeled, cooked potatoes; 2 cups chopped unpared apple; and 2 tablespoons thinly sliced green onion. Blend together 1 cup dairy sour cream, 2 tablespoons lemon juice, ½ teaspoon salt, ¼ teaspoon dillweed, and dash pepper; toss lightly with potato mixture. Chill. Serves 10 to 12.

COTTAGE SHELL SALAD

Cook 2 cups shell macaroni following package directions; drain. Stir in 2 cups cottage cheese, ¼ cup *each* diced canned pimiento, snipped chives, and sliced radishes. Blend 1 cup dairy sour cream, ¼ cup French salad dressing, 2 tablespoons lemon juice, ½ teaspoon *each* salt and dry mustard. Toss with macaroni. Chill. Serves 10.

DEVILED POTATO SALAD

Cut 8 hard-cooked eggs in half. Remove yolks and mash; blend with 3 tablespoons vinegar and 3 tablespoons prepared mustard. Stir in 1 cup mayonnaise or salad dressing, ½ cup dairy sour cream, 1 teaspoon salt, and ½ teaspoon celery salt; mix well.

Chop egg whites; combine with 6 medium potatoes, cooked, peeled, and cubed, and 2 tablespoons chopped onion. Fold in egg yolk mixture; chill. Garnish with tomato wedges and cucumber slices. Serves 6 to 8.

SWISS POTATO SALAD

      4 cups cubed, peeled, cooked
          potatoes
      1 teaspoon salt
      4 slices (4 ounces) Swiss cheese,
          cut in narrow strips
      1 cup dairy sour cream
      3 tablespoons milk
      2 tablespoons snipped chives *or*
          chopped green onion
      ½ teaspoon dry mustard

Sprinkle salt over potatoes; combine with cheese strips. Blend remaining ingredients; pour over potato mixture. Toss lightly. Serve at room temperature. Serves 4 or 5.

MASHED POTATO SALAD

      4 medium potatoes, pared
      ¾ cup mayonnaise or salad
          dressing
      2 tablespoons vinegar
      1½ teaspoons celery salt
      ⅓ cup chopped sweet pickle
      ¼ cup chopped celery
      ¼ cup finely chopped onion
      4 hard-cooked eggs, sliced
      2 tablespoons chopped canned
          pimiento

In medium saucepan, cook potatoes in boiling salted water till tender. Drain and mash. Combine mayonnaise, vinegar, celery salt, and dash pepper; stir into hot mashed potatoes. Add pickle, celery, and onion; mix well. Fold in hard-cooked eggs and pimiento. Serve warm or chilled. Serves 8 to 10.

EASY POTATO SALAD

      2 9-ounce packages frozen French-
          fried potatoes
      1½ teaspoons salt
      ⅔ cup coarsely grated unpared
          cucumber
      ½ cup sliced radishes
      ½ cup diced celery
      2 tablespoons sliced green onion
      2 tablespoons snipped parsley
      1 cup mayonnaise or salad
          dressing
      1 to 2 tablespoons vinegar
                  •   •   •
      2 hard-cooked eggs, sliced
      Paprika

Pour 4 cups water into large saucepan; bring to rapid boil. Carefully drop frozen potatoes into water. Remove from heat immediately; cover and let stand 4 to 5 minutes. Drain potatoes at once, and spread onto paper toweling. Sprinkle with salt; cool. Blend together remaining ingredients *except* eggs and paprika. Add potatoes and toss. Chill. Garnish with eggs and paprika. Serves 10 to 12.

MACARONI-BEAN SALAD

Cook ½ of 7-ounce package elbow macaroni (about 1 cup) following package directions. Drain well and cool. Combine cooked macaroni; one 8-ounce can kidney beans, drained; 2 hard-cooked eggs, chopped; and ¼ cup pickle relish.

Blend together ½ cup mayonnaise or salad dressing, ½ teaspoon salt, and 3 drops bottled hot pepper sauce; toss lightly with macaroni mixture. Chill. Serves 6 to 8.

POTATO SALAD CUPS

Combine 6 cups cubed, peeled, cooked potatoes; 1 medium unpared cucumber, diced (2 cups); 1 cup chopped celery; 3 hard-cooked eggs, sliced; ½ cup chopped onion; 1½ teaspoons salt; and ¼ teaspoon paprika. Pour ¼ cup French salad dressing with herbs and spices over. Chill. Combine ½ cup mayonnaise and 1 teaspoon celery seed. Add to potato mixture; toss lightly. Pack into custard cups; unmold on lettuce. Serves 8.

WAYS WITH BEANS

ONE BEAN TOSS

½ cup sliced pitted ripe olives
¼ cup sliced pimiento-stuffed
   green olives
1 16-ounce can peas, drained
1 16-ounce can limas, drained
½ cup mayonnaise
2 tablespoons grated onion
1 tablespoon lemon juice
1 tablespoon drained capers
2 teaspoons liquid from capers
   Herbed Carrots
   Parsley

Set aside a few olive slices for garnish; combine remaining olive slices, peas, and limas in bowl. Combine next 5 ingredients, ½ teaspoon salt, and dash pepper; pour over bean mixture and toss lightly. Cover; chill several hours, stirring occasionally. To serve, mound salad in center of lettuce-lined platter. Top with reserved olives and additional mayonnaise, if desired. Arrange Herbed Carrots and parsley around. Serves 8.

Herbed Carrots: Place one 16-ounce can whole small carrots, drained, in a deep bowl. Combine ⅓ cup salad oil; 2 tablespoons tarragon vinegar; 2 tablespoons finely snipped parsley; ¼ teaspoon salt; ¼ teaspoon dried thyme leaves, crushed, *or* dried marjoram leaves, crushed; and dash pepper. Pour over carrots. Cover; chill 3 hours, spooning dressing over occasionally. Drain.

HOT FIVE BEAN SALAD

In large skillet, cook 8 slices bacon till crisp; drain, reserving ¼ cup drippings. Crumble bacon; set aside. In skillet, combine ⅔ cup sugar, 2 tablespoons cornstarch, 1½ teaspoons salt, and dash pepper with reserved drippings. Stir in ¾ cup vinegar and ½ cup water; heat to boiling, stirring constantly. Add one 16-ounce can *each* kidney beans, cut green beans, limas, cut wax beans, and garbanzo beans, *all drained.* Reduce heat. Cover; simmer 15 to 20 minutes. Turn into dish. Top with bacon. Serves 10 to 12.

FOUR BEAN SALAD

Want applauds and cheers for a good-tasting salad? Try this delicious combination—

   Romaine leaves
   • • •
1 16-ounce can red kidney beans,
   drained
1 16-ounce can cut wax
   beans, drained
1 16-ounce can black-eyed peas
   or limas, drained
1 16-ounce can cut green beans,
   drained
1 medium green pepper, thinly
   sliced into rings
1 medium onion, thinly sliced
   and separated into rings
   • • •
½ cup sugar
½ cup wine vinegar
½ cup salad oil
2 tablespoons snipped parsley
1 teaspoon salt
½ teaspoon dry mustard
½ teaspoon dried tarragon
   leaves, crushed, *or* 2
   teaspoons finely snipped
   fresh tarragon
½ teaspoon dried basil leaves,
   crushed, *or* 2 teaspoons
   finely snipped fresh basil

Line large salad bowl with romaine. Layer drained red kidney beans, wax beans, black-eyed peas, green beans, and pepper rings in order given. Top with onion rings. Thoroughly combine sugar, vinegar, oil, parsley, salt, dry mustard, tarragon, and basil. Drizzle over vegetables. Cover; chill thoroughly, stirring occasionally. Just before serving, stir; then drain. Makes 12 servings.

Surprise and please bean lovers with these →
salads. Herbed Carrots add tempting appeal to
One Bean Toss. Hot Five Bean Salad and Four
Bean Salad are hearty main dish selections.

ITALIAN BEAN TOSS

Sprightly seasoned with Parmesan and curry—

> 2 9-ounce packages frozen Italian
>   green beans
> ½ cup mayonnaise or salad
>   dressing
> 2 tablespoons grated Parmesan
>   cheese
> 1 tablespoon finely chopped
>   canned pimiento
> ¼ teaspoon curry powder

Cook beans following package directions; drain and chill. Blend together mayonnaise, Parmesan, pimiento, curry, and 1 teaspoon salt. Add beans and toss; chill. If desired, sprinkle with additional Parmesan cheese before serving. Makes 6 to 8 servings.

KIDNEY BEAN CLASSIC

Hard cook 3 eggs; chop 2 eggs and slice remaining for garnish. Combine one 16-ounce can kidney beans, drained; ¾ cup chopped celery; ¼ cup chopped sweet pickle; the 2 chopped eggs; and 1 tablespoon chopped onion. Blend ½ cup mayonnaise, 2 teaspoons prepared mustard, and ½ teaspoon salt. Add mayonnaise mixture to bean mixture and toss. Arrange the sliced hard-cooked egg atop salad. Chill. Makes 6 servings.

EGG AND BEAN SALAD

> 1 16-ounce can barbecue beans,
>   drained
> 6 hard-cooked eggs, coarsely
>   chopped
> ¼ cup chopped onion
> 1 tablespoon mayonnaise or salad
>   dressing
> 1 teaspoon prepared mustard
> ¼ teaspoon salt
> 3 slices bacon, crisp-cooked and
>   crumbled

Combine beans, eggs, and onion. Chill. Blend together mayonnaise, mustard, salt, and dash pepper. Add to egg mixture and toss. Spoon into lettuce-lined salad bowl. Sprinkle bacon over top. Makes 6 to 8 servings.

CREAMY LIMA CUPS

Cook one 10-ounce package frozen baby limas following package directions; drain and chill well. Blend together ¼ cup dairy sour cream; 1 tablespoon vinegar; 1 tablespoon salad oil; 1 small clove garlic, minced; ½ teaspoon sugar; ¼ teaspoon salt; and dash paprika. Add chilled beans and toss. Spoon into 4 lettuce cups. Sprinkle with additional paprika. Makes 4 servings.

HOT BEAN SALAD

> 1 16-ounce can kidney beans,
>   drained
> 1 cup thinly sliced celery
> 3 ounces sharp process American
>   cheese, diced (¾ cup)
> ⅓ cup chopped sweet pickle
> ¼ cup thinly sliced green onion
> ½ cup mayonnaise or salad
>   dressing
> ⅓ cup finely crushed rich round
>   cracker crumbs

Combine first 6 ingredients and ¼ teaspoon salt; toss. Spoon into four 8-ounce bakers or six 5-ounce custard cups. Top with crumbs. Bake in very hot oven (450°) for 10 minutes or till bubbly. Makes 4 to 6 servings.

CHILI-BEAN SALAD

Zestful salad from the Southwest—

> 2 16-ounce cans green beans,
>   drained and chilled
> ¾ cup diced celery
> ¼ cup small white onion rings
> 2 tablespoons pickle relish
>   Chili Salad Dressing

Combine first 4 ingredients and ½ teaspoon salt. Add Chili Salad Dressing; toss. Cover and chill at least 1 hour. Serves 6 to 8.

Chili Salad Dressing: Combine 2 tablespoons salad oil, ½ small clove garlic, ¼ teaspoon chili powder, ⅛ teaspoon salt, and dash pepper. Let stand 1 hour. Remove and discard garlic. Add 1 tablespoon vinegar and 1½ teaspoons lemon juice; beat with rotary beater. Chill thoroughly.

"Make-ahead" recipes end the last minute mealtime rush. Tomato-bean Combo not only falls into this category but also takes little prepara-tion time. The vegetable mixture is evenly coated with a tingling sour cream and Italian dressing blend. Tomato wedges are the colorful garnish.

TOMATO-BEAN COMBO

  1 16-ounce can cut green beans, drained
  2 medium tomatoes, peeled, chopped, and drained (about 1½ cups)
  ¼ cup finely chopped onion
  ½ cup dairy sour cream
  ¼ cup Italian salad dressing
    Romaine leaves
    Tomato wedges

Combine cut green beans, chopped tomato, and chopped onion. Blend together sour cream and Italian salad dressing; add to bean mixture and toss lightly. Chill at least 2 to 3 hours. At serving time, spoon salad into romaine-lined salad bowl. Garnish with to-mato wedges. Makes 6 servings.

MARINATED BEAN SALAD

  1 16-ounce can cut green beans
  1 16-ounce can cut yellow wax beans
  ⅔ cup vinegar
  1 teaspoon mixed pickling spices
    Non-caloric liquid sweetener equal to ¼ cup sugar
  ½ cup chopped celery
  2 slices bacon, crisp-cooked and crumbled

Drain beans, reserving ½ cup liquid. Heat bean liquid with vinegar, ⅓ cup water, and spices. Boil 2 to 3 minutes. Cool and strain. Stir in sweetener. Combine beans and celery; add dressing. Cover and chill 6 hours or over-night, stirring occasionally. Before serving, top with bacon. Makes 8 servings.

VARIATIONS WITH VEGETABLES

ASPARAGUS-TOMATO SALAD

  2 pounds fresh asparagus spears,
     cooked and drained
1/3 cup mayonnaise
1 1/4 teaspoons lemon juice
  1 medium tomato, peeled and
     diced

Keep asparagus hot. In small saucepan, combine mayonnaise, lemon juice, 1/4 teaspoon salt, and 1/8 teaspoon pepper. Stir over low heat till heated through. Stir in tomato; heat through. Serve over asparagus. Serves 6.

MEDITERRANEAN SALAD

  1 10-ounce package frozen
     Italian green beans
  2 tablespoons butter or margarine
  3 slices bread, cut in cubes
     (2 cups)
  1 12-ounce can whole kernel corn,
     drained
1/2 cup mayonnaise or salad
     dressing
  2 tablespoons chopped canned
     pimiento
  1 teaspoon dried basil leaves,
     crushed

Cook beans following package directions; drain and cool. In skillet, melt butter. Add bread cubes and cook till crisp, turning occasionally. Combine beans, corn, mayonnaise, pimiento, basil, and 1/4 teaspoon salt; chill. Before serving, add toasted bread cubes to bean mixture; toss. Serves 8.

← A magnificent vegetable mixture awaiting all salad lovers—that's Mediterranean Salad. Italian beans, corn, and pimiento team up with crunchy toasted bread cubes in this savory special.

CALICO RICE SALAD

  3 cups cooked rice
  6 hard-cooked eggs, coarsely
     chopped
1/2 cup chopped onion
1/4 cup chopped canned pimiento
1/4 cup chopped green pepper
1/4 cup chopped celery
1/4 cup chopped dill pickle
1/3 cup mayonnaise or salad
     dressing
1/4 cup French salad dressing
  2 tablespoons prepared mustard

Combine rice, eggs, onion, pimiento, green pepper, celery, dill pickle, 1 teaspoon salt, and dash pepper. Blend together mayonnaise, French salad dressing, and mustard; add to rice mixture and toss. Chill thoroughly. Lightly pack rice mixture into five 5-ounce custard cups; immediately turn out on lettuce-lined plates. Makes 5 servings.

ENDIVE-AVOCADO SALAD

  8 French endives
  1 avocado, halved, peeled, and
     sliced
  4 scallions *or* green onions,
     chopped
1/4 cup salad oil
  1 tablespoon wine vinegar
  2 tablespoons snipped parsley

Chill endive in ice water to crisp. Dry gently with paper toweling. Remove a few outer leaves and set aside. Cut endive stalks into large crosswise slices. In salad bowl, combine endive slices, avocado, and scallions. Season to taste with salt and pepper.

Combine salad oil and vinegar; pour over endive mixture and toss lightly. Top with parsley. Arrange reserved endive leaves around edge of bowl. Makes 6 servings.

PIQUANT CAULIFLOWER

A creative treatment of a vinaigrette—

  1 medium head cauliflower
  ⅔ cup salad oil
  ⅓ cup white vinegar
  1 large tomato, chopped
  2 tablespoons chopped pimiento-
      stuffed green olives
  1 tablespoon pickle relish
  1 teaspoon sugar
  1 teaspoon salt
  1 teaspoon paprika
  ⅛ teaspoon pepper

Separate cauliflower into flowerets. Cook, covered, in small amount of boiling salted water just till crisp-tender, about 10 minutes; drain. Place cauliflowerets in deep bowl. Combine remaining ingredients. Pour over cauliflower and chill 2 to 3 hours, stirring occasionally. At serving time, drain off excess oil-vinegar mixture. Serve in lettuce-lined bowl. Makes 8 servings.

SWEDISH VEGETABLES

LOW CALORIE · LOW CALORIE

  1 10-ounce package frozen
      cauliflower
  1 16-ounce can *each* shoestring
      carrots, drained; cut green
      beans, drained; and peas,
      drained
  1 15-ounce can artichoke hearts,
      drained and halved
  1 cup chopped celery
  ½ cup low-calorie French-style
      salad dressing
  1 tablespoon instant minced onion
      Chili-dill Dressing

Cook cauliflower according to package directions; drain well. Cool and separate into flowerets. Arrange vegetables in large salad bowl. Combine French-style salad dressing and onion. Drizzle over vegetables; chill 1 hour. Serve with Chili-dill Dressing. Makes 10 to 12 servings.

Chili-dill Dressing: Blend ¾ cup low-calorie mayonnaise-type dressing with ¼ cup chili sauce, 2 teaspoons dried dillweed, 1 teaspoon salt, dash pepper, and 1 tablespoon lemon juice. Chill thoroughly.

VEGETABLE COMBO

For a speedy salad, use canned vegatables—

  ½ cup peas, cooked and drained
  ½ cup baby limas, cooked and
      drained
  ½ cup finely diced carrot
  ½ cup bias-cut celery
  ½ cup paper-thin onion slices
      Dairy sour cream
  10 to 20 capers

Combine all ingredients *except* sour cream and capers. Chill thoroughly. Serve on lettuce-lined plates. Spoon sour cream over. Garnish with capers. Makes 6 servings.

PANAMA RADISH SALAD

  1½ cups sliced radishes
  1 cup finely diced tomato
  ¼ cup thinly sliced onion rings
      . . .
  2 tablespoons salad oil
  2 tablespoons lemon juice
  2 teaspoons snipped parsley
  ½ teaspoon salt
  ⅛ teaspoon garlic salt
  ⅛ teaspoon black pepper

Combine radishes, tomato, and onion. In screw-top jar, shake together remaining ingredients. Pour over radish mixture; toss. Chill 1 hour. Makes 4 or 5 servings.

HERBED PEA SALAD

Dill is the fragrant herb used—

  2 10-ounce packages frozen peas
  ⅓ cup clear French salad dressing
      with herbs and spices
  ½ teaspoon dried dillweed
  1 cup thinly sliced celery
  1 hard-cooked egg, sliced

Cook peas according to package directions; drain. Combine clear French salad dressing with dillweed; pour over peas and celery. Chill several hours or overnight, stirring occasionally. Serve in lettuce-lined bowl. Top with hard-cooked egg slices. Serves 6 to 8.

VEGETABLE MARINADE

1 medium head cauliflower
1 16-ounce can whole green beans,
   drained
⅔ cup salad oil
⅓ cup vinegar
1 envelope onion salad dressing
   mix

Separate cauliflower into small flowerets. Cook, covered, in small amount of boiling salted water till crisp-tender, about 10 minutes; drain well. Place hot cauliflower and beans in bowl. In screw-top jar, combine oil, vinegar, and salad dressing mix; cover and shake well. Pour dressing over vegetables; chill several hours or overnight, stirring occasionally. Drain; serve vegetables on lettuce-lined plates. Makes 4 to 6 servings.

ZUCCHINI VINAIGRETTE

The zucchini tastes like Italian pickles—

¼ cup sauterne
1 envelope Italian salad dressing
   mix
½ cup salad *or* olive oil
¼ cup white wine vinegar
3 to 4 tablespoons finely sliced
   green onion
3 tablespoons drained
   pickle relish
2 tablespoons finely snipped
   parsley
2 tablespoons finely chopped
   green pepper
5 or 6 medium zucchini
3 or 4 medium tomatoes, chilled
   and sliced

For dressing, combine wine and dressing mix in screw-top jar; cover and shake. Add salad oil and next 5 ingredients.

Slice each zucchini in 6 lengthwise strips. Cook in boiling salted water just till tender, about 3 to 5 minutes. Drain; arrange in shallow dish. Shake dressing and pour over zucchini. Cover and refrigerate several hours or overnight, spooning dressing over occasionally. To serve, drain zucchini and arrange on lettuce-lined platter with tomatoes. Makes 8 or 9 servings.

MEXICAN SALAD

2 medium tomatoes, cut in chunks
1 large green pepper, cut in
   ½-inch chunks
¼ cup chopped celery
2 tablespoons sliced green onion
2 slices bacon, crisp-cooked
   and crumbled
2 hard-cooked eggs, sliced
       . . .
¼ cup vinegar
¼ teaspoon salt
¼ teaspoon chili powder

Combine first 6 ingredients. Heat vinegar, salt, and chili powder to boiling. Pour over vegetable mixture; toss. Makes 4 servings.

VEGETABLE MEDLEY

Combine 2 cups chopped cucumbers, 1 cup sliced radishes, and 1 cup sliced green onions with tops. Blend together ½ cup dairy sour cream, 1 tablespoon lemon juice, ½ teaspoon salt, and ⅛ teaspoon dry mustard; toss lightly with vegetable mixture. Chill. Serve on lettuce-lined plate. Serves 4 to 6.

Cucumber Medley: Prepare recipe for Vegetable Medley *except* use 1½ cups sliced cucumbers in place of chopped cucumbers, radishes, and green onions.

FILLED TOMATO ROSETTES

4 medium tomatoes
¼ teaspoon salt
1 avocado, peeled and diced
1 8-ounce carton (1 cup) cream-
   style cottage cheese, drained
¼ cup dairy sour cream
1 tablespoon snipped chives *or*
   chopped green onion tops

With stem end down, cut each tomato into 6 wedges, *cutting to, but not through,* base of tomato. Spread wedges apart slightly. Sprinkle with salt; chill. In small mixing bowl, blend avocado and next 2 ingredients together. Fill each tomato with about ⅓ cup avocado mixture. Top with chives or green onion tops. Makes 4 servings.

VEGETABLES TO BRIGHTEN BUFFETS

VEGETABLE SALAD TRAY

Sour Cream Potato Toss (see below)
Fresh or frozen asparagus spears, cooked, drained, and chilled
Tomatoes, cut in wedges
Raw zucchini, bias-cut

Mound Sour Cream Potato Toss in center of large lettuce-lined tray. Sieve reserved egg yolk over. Arrange asparagus, tomatoes, and zucchini on tray around potato salad.

SOUR CREAM POTATO TOSS

6 cups diced, peeled, cooked potatoes
1/4 cup chopped green onions with tops
1 1/2 teaspoons salt
1 teaspoon celery seed
4 hard-cooked eggs
1 cup dairy sour cream
1/2 cup mayonnaise
2 tablespoons vinegar
1 teaspoon prepared mustard
3/4 cup diced pared cucumber

Combine first 4 ingredients and 1/8 teaspoon pepper. Separate whites of hard-cooked eggs from yolks; chop whites and add to potato mixture. Chill thoroughly.

Reserve 1 hard-cooked yolk. To prepare dressing, mash remaining yolks; blend in sour cream, mayonnaise, vinegar, and mustard. Pour dressing over potato mixture; toss lightly. Let stand 20 minutes. Just before serving, fold in cucumber. Sieve reserved hard-cooked yolk over. Serves 10 to 12.

Curried Potato Toss: Prepare Sour Cream Potato Toss omitting mustard; add 1/2 to 1 teaspoon curry powder to dressing mixture.

COLESLAW HAWAIIAN

Is a pleasing balance of sweet and sassy—

In very large bowl, dissolve six 3-ounce packages lemon-flavored gelatin in 7 cups boiling water. Stir in 3 tablespoons lemon juice. Chill till partially set. Beat in 1 1/2 cups dairy sour cream till smooth.

Fold in 2 quarts (8 cups) chopped cabbage, two 20 1/2-ounce cans undrained crushed pineapple, and 1/3 cup chopped green pepper. Pour into 18x12x2-inch pan. Chill till firm. Makes 30 (1/2 cup) servings.

AVOCADO-VEGETABLE TOSS

Lots of hearty distinction—

2 12-ounce cans whole kernel corn, drained and chilled
2 medium avocados, peeled and diced
6 hard-cooked eggs, diced and chilled
2 tablespoons chopped onion
1 cup mayonnaise or salad dressing
1 tablespoon lemon juice
1/2 teaspoon chili powder
1/4 teaspoon ground cumin
1/8 teaspoon ground nutmeg

Combine corn, avocados, eggs, and onion. Blend together remaining ingredients. Toss mayonnaise mixture lightly with avocado mixture. Garnish with sliced pitted ripe olives, if desired. Makes 8 to 10 servings.

Guests will return to the buffet table for second helpings of Vegetable Salad Tray. A colorful splash of asparagus, tomato, and zucchini encompasses a mound of zippy Sour Cream Potato Toss.

VEGETABLE SALAD WREATH

Arrange crisp salad greens on large platter. Set Starlight Molds around outer rim; tuck two 10-ounce packages asparagus spears, cooked, drained, and chilled, in between molds. Break 1 small head raw cauliflower into flowerets; slice and arrange with two 16-ounce cans small whole carrots, drained and chilled, in inner circle. Place cherry tomatoes and greens in center. Serve with French salad dressing. Makes 14 servings.

Starlight Molds: Dissolve two 3-ounce packages lemon-flavored gelatin in 2 cups boiling water. Add 2 cups cold water and 2 tablespoons lemon juice. Chill *1 cup* gelatin till partially set; fold in 1 cup shredded cabbage and 1 tablespoon chopped canned pimiento. Divide among six ½-cup molds. Chill till *almost* firm.

Chill remaining gelatin till partially set; fold in 2 cups shredded carrots. Fill eight ½-cup molds. Spoon remaining gelatin over partially-filled molds. Chill till firm. Unmold; top with pimiento stars. Makes 14.

MEAL-ON-A-PLATTER

3 cups whole green beans, cooked and drained
1½ cups peas, cooked and drained
1 cup garlic salad dressing
1 12-ounce carton (1½ cups) cream-style cottage cheese
Snipped chives
4 large lettuce cups
12 celery strips
12 carrot curls
1 12-ounce can luncheon meat, cut in thin strips
Canned pimiento strips

Place beans and peas in separate dishes; pour dressing over. Chill 2 hours, spooning dressing over occasionally; drain. Center bowl of chive-topped cottage cheese on platter. Arrange lettuce cups around bowl; fill one with peas, one with celery, one with carrots, and one with meat. Arrange beans between cups; top with pimiento. Pass extra dressing. Makes 6 servings.

Decorate the party buffet table with a Vegetable Salad Wreath. The platter, lined with perky salad greens, is centered with an array of vegetables. Individual serving-size molds around the outside are filled with crisp shredded cabbage and carrot and garnished with colorful pimiento stars.

THREE SALAD ENSEMBLE

Arrange 3 large lettuce cups in shallow bowl. Fill one with Herbed Tomato Slices, one with Relish Cottage Cheese, and one with Oriental Relish. Garnish with parsley sprigs and cucumber slices.

HERBED TOMATO SLICES

    ⅓ cup salad oil
    2 tablespoons tarragon vinegar
    ½ teaspoon salt
    ¼ teaspoon dried thyme leaves, crushed
    ¼ teaspoon dried marjoram leaves, crushed
    3 tomatoes, peeled and sliced

Combine first 5 ingredients and dash pepper. Pour over tomatoes in shallow bowl. Chill 2 to 3 hours, spooning dressing over tomatoes occasionally; drain. Makes 4 cups.

RELISH COTTAGE CHEESE

    1 12-ounce carton (1½ cups) cream-style cottage cheese, drained
    2 tablespoons chopped canned pimiento
    1 to 2 tablespoons chopped green onions *or* chives
    1 to 2 tablespoons chopped green pepper
    1 teaspoon prepared horseradish
    ¼ teaspoon salt

Combine ingredients; chill. Makes 2 cups.

ORIENTAL RELISH

Sprinkle 2 cups paper-thin cucumber slices with ½ teaspoon salt; chill. Drain in sieve, pressing with paper towels to remove excess moisture. Sprinkle 2 cups shredded carrots with ¼ teaspoon salt.

Dissolve ½ cup sugar in ½ cup white vinegar. Place cucumber slices and carrots in separate dishes. Pour vinegar mixture over. Chill at least 1 hour. Before serving, drain. Heap cucumber in center of lettuce cup; circle with carrots. Makes 3½ cups.

TOSSED GREEN SALAD

    3 heads (1½ to 2 pounds each) lettuce
    1 bunch romaine (½ pound)
    2 bunches radishes, sliced
    2 large cucumbers, thinly sliced (4 cups)
    2 large green peppers, chopped
    1 large onion, chopped (optional)
    1 pint French salad dressing
    ⅔ cup sweet pickle relish
    ⅓ cup vinegar

Tear lettuce and romaine in bite-size pieces and layer in several large salad bowls with next 4 ingredients; chill. Combine remaining ingredients; before serving, toss with vegetables. Makes 25 (about 1 cup) servings.

SALAD WHEEL

    1 bunch leaf lettuce
      Pitted green and ripe olives
    4 large tomatoes, sliced
    2 raw turnips, sliced
    1 medium unpared cucumber, sliced
   10 radish roses
      Green onions with tops
      Whole sweet pickles
      Parsley sprigs
      Green pepper rings

Arrange lettuce leaves on serving platter. Place olives in center of platter. Form 6 vegetable "spokes" by alternating slices of tomato, turnip, and cucumber. Arrange groupings of radishes, onions, and pickles between spokes. Garnish with sprigs of parsley and green pepper rings.

CABBAGE SLAW

Combine 2¼ pounds cabbage, shredded (15 cups); ¾ pound carrots, shredded (3 cups); and ¾ cup diced green pepper; chill. Blend 3 cups mayonnaise or salad dressing, ⅓ cup sugar, ⅓ cup vinegar, 1 tablespoon prepared mustard, 3 teaspoons celery seed, and 2 teaspoons salt. Just before serving, toss vegetables and mayonnaise mixture lightly. Makes 25 (½ cup) servings.

SALAD ENTREES

Looking for a menu for that next luncheon or late evening supper? Plan the meal around a salad. All that needs to be added is a bread, beverage, and luscious dessert.

Lightly tossed salad bowls head the list of this idea-packed chapter. To keep salad bowls cool, place the bowl in a bed of crushed ice (as seen at left). Or, prepare individual salad bowls and serve in icers.

If one fancies gelatin salads that are made ahead, choose a molded main dish salad. It will eliminate much of the last-minute fuss. Then, when the serving hour arrives, just unmold on a lettuce-lined plate.

Suggestions abound for presenting main dish salads attractively. Impressive meals are easy to plan around these delightful entrees.

When the temperature soars and appetites are on the wane, serve Ham and Cheese Medley. Two "old-favorites" are teamed with fruit, then capped with sour cream.

MEALS IN A BOWL

HAM AND CHEESE MEDLEY

1 8¾-ounce can pineapple tidbits
1 small head lettuce, torn in
    bite-size pieces (4 cups)
1 cup cubed fully-cooked ham
1 cup halved seedless green grapes
2 ounces natural Swiss cheese,
    cut in strips
  Bibb lettuce
1 cup dairy sour cream

Drain pineapple, reserving ¼ cup syrup. Toss together pineapple and next 4 ingredients. Line salad bowl with Bibb lettuce; spoon in salad mixture. Chill. For dressing, stir reserved syrup into sour cream till well blended; chill. To serve, spoon a little dressing atop salad. Garnish with additional green grapes and Bibb lettuce, if desired. Pass remaining dressing. Makes 6 servings.

DEVILED BEEF TOSS

1 head romaine, torn in bite-size
    pieces
3 cups torn lettuce
1½ cups cooked roast beef cut
    in strips
12 cherry tomatoes
½ medium onion, sliced and
    separated into rings
1 2-ounce can rolled anchovy
    fillets, drained
  Mustard-horseradish Dressing

In large bowl, toss greens together. Arrange beef strips, cherry tomatoes, onion rings, and anchovies on greens. Serve with Mustard-horseradish Dressing. Makes 6 servings.

Mustard-horseradish Dressing: In small bowl, combine 1 tablespoon sugar, 1 teaspoon salt, 1 teaspoon dry mustard, ¼ teaspoon white pepper, and dash paprika. Add 1 tablespoon horseradish and ½ teaspoon grated onion. With electric mixer at medium speed, slowly add ⅔ cup salad oil, a little at a time, alternately with ⅓ cup white wine vinegar. Chill thoroughly.

SALAMI-CHEESE SALAD

6 cups torn lettuce
1 cup sliced salami cut in
    quarters
4 ounces natural Swiss cheese,
    cut in strips
½ cup sliced pitted ripe olives
3 tablespoons chopped canned
    pimiento
1 2-ounce can anchovy fillets,
    drained and chopped
⅓ cup salad oil
3 tablespoons wine vinegar
½ clove garlic, crushed

Combine lettuce, salami, cheese, olives, pimiento, and anchovies. In screw-top jar, combine oil, vinegar, and garlic for dressing. Cover; shake well. Pour dressing over salad and toss lightly. Makes 8 servings.

HAM-CHICKEN SUPREME

6 cups torn lettuce
1 cup diced cucumber
1 medium green pepper, cut in
    narrow strips
1 cup fully-cooked ham cut
    in strips
1 cup cooked chicken cut
    in strips
3 hard-cooked eggs, sliced
2 medium tomatoes, cut in wedges
   . . .
½ cup salad oil
3 tablespoons vinegar
1 tablespoon prepared horseradish
½ teaspoon Worcestershire sauce
2 drops bottled hot pepper sauce
½ teaspoon salt
⅛ teaspoon pepper

Line individual salad bowls with lettuce. Arrange cucumber, green pepper, ham, chicken, eggs, and tomatoes in each. In screw-top jar, combine remaining ingredients for dressing. Cover and shake well. Pass dressing with salads. Makes 8 to 10 servings.

TUNA-CREAM PUFF BOWL

   4 hard-cooked eggs
   1 9¼-ounce can tuna, drained
   1 tablespoon lemon juice
   1 cup sliced celery
  ¼ cup sliced pimiento-stuffed
      green olives
  ¼ cup finely chopped onion
  ½ cup mayonnaise
      Cream Puff Bowl
   2 cups shredded lettuce

Sieve 1 egg yolk and slice 1 whole egg; reserve for garnish. Coarsely chop remaining eggs and white. Break tuna in chunks; sprinkle with lemon juice. Add next 3 ingredients, ¼ teaspoon salt, and dash pepper. Fold in mayonnaise and chopped eggs; chill. Just before serving, cover bottom of Cream Puff Bowl with lettuce; fill with tuna salad. Garnish with egg slices and sieved yolk. Serves 6.

CREAM PUFF BOWL

  ¼ cup butter or margarine
  ½ cup boiling water
  ½ cup sifted all-purpose flour
  ¼ teaspoon celery seed
   2 eggs

In 1-quart saucepan, melt butter in boiling water. Add flour, celery seed, and dash salt all at once; stir vigorously. Cook, stirring constantly, over low heat till mixture forms a ball that doesn't separate. Remove from heat and cool slightly. Add eggs, one at a time, beating vigorously after each till smooth. Spread batter evenly over bottom and sides of greased 9-inch pie plate. Bake in very hot oven (450°) 15 minutes; reduce oven temperature to 325° and bake 30 minutes longer. Turn oven off (keep oven door closed) and let puff dry out, about 20 minutes. Remove from oven and cool on rack.

Fascinate guests and family alike with Tuna-cream Puff Bowl. A baked salad bowl to be eaten along with the crunchy salad adds to the fun. Since the ingredients are usually right at hand, there's no need to wait for a special occasion. The compliments make it worth any extra preparation time.

LEMON CAPER CRAB SALAD

LOW CALORIE · LOW CALORIE

        2 6-ounce packages frozen crab
          meat, thawed
        1 10-ounce package frozen
          asparagus spears, cooked,
          drained, and chilled
                • • •
        ½ cup low-calorie mayonnaise-
          type dressing
        1 tablespoon lemon juice
        1 teaspoon drained capers
        ½ teaspoon prepared mustard
        ½ teaspoon Worcestershire sauce
        3 hard-cooked eggs, sliced

Break crab into chunks, removing cartilage.
Place 3 asparagus spears on each of 6 lettuce-
lined plates and ⅓ cup crab meat over asparagus. Blend together remaining ingredients
except eggs. Spoon 1 tablespoon mayonnaise
mixture atop crab. Trim with hard-cooked
egg slices. Makes 6 servings.

MEAT AND BEAN SALAD

        1 cup cubed cooked meat
        1 8-ounce can kidney beans,
          drained
        ½ cup sliced celery
        1 hard-cooked egg, chopped
        3 tablespoons chopped onion
        1 tablespoon sweet pickle relish
        ⅓ cup mayonnaise
        1 tablespoon chili sauce

Combine first 6 ingredients. To prepare
dressing, blend together mayonnaise, chili
sauce, and ¼ teaspoon salt. Toss dressing
with meat mixture; chill. Serves 3 or 4.

TUNA-MELON DINNER SALAD

Combine 4 cups torn lettuce (about ½
large head); 2 cups cubed cantaloupe; one
11-ounce can mandarin oranges, drained;
one 6½- or 7-ounce can tuna, drained and
flaked; ¾ cup sliced process American cheese
cut in strips; ½ cup chopped celery; ¼ cup
sliced green onion; and ¼ cup sliced pitted
ripe olives. Blend ½ cup mayonnaise or salad
dressing and 1 tablespoon lemon juice; add
to tuna mixture and toss lightly. Serves 8.

MACARONI SALMON SALAD

        ¾ cup uncooked elbow macaroni
        1 7¾-ounce can salmon, drained
          and flaked
        ¾ cup chopped celery
        2 tablespoons chopped onion
        ¾ cup mayonnaise or salad
          dressing
        ¼ teaspoon liquid smoke
          Parsley

Cook macaroni following package directions;
drain. Combine macaroni, salmon, celery,
and onion. Blend mayonnaise, liquid smoke,
and ¼ teaspoon salt; toss lightly with salmon mixture. Chill. Garnish with parsley.
Makes 3 or 4 servings.

DUBLIN POTATO SALAD

        2 tablespoons vinegar
        1 teaspoon celery seed
        1 teaspoon mustard seed
        3 medium-large potatoes
        2 teaspoons sugar
        2 cups finely shredded cabbage
        1 12-ounce can corned beef,
          chilled and cubed
        ¼ cup sliced green onion
        ¼ cup finely chopped dill pickle
        1 cup mayonnaise or salad
          dressing
        ¼ cup milk

Combine vinegar, celery seed, and mustard
seed; set aside. Meanwhile, pare and cook
potatoes in enough boiling salted water to
cover for 30 to 40 minutes or till done; drain
and cube. While potatoes are still warm,
drizzle with vinegar mixture. Sprinkle with
sugar and ½ teaspoon salt; chill.

Before serving, add cabbage, corned beef,
onion, and pickle to potatoes. Combine mayonnaise, milk, and ½ teaspoon salt. Pour
mayonnaise mixture over corned beef mixture and toss lightly. Serves 6 to 8.

It's the luck o' the Irish when portions of →
Dublin Potato Salad are served. The familiar
corned beef and cabbage combination with
potato welcomes a peppy sweet-tart dressing.

Think "fast and easy" when preparing Skillet Chef's Salad. Strips of hearty ham and cheese, hard-cooked egg slices, lettuce, and an assortment of vegetables are heated in a sassy sweet-sour dressing. The menu is complete when served with piping-hot muffins, jam or jelly, and beverage.

SKILLET CHEF'S SALAD

In medium skillet, blend 2 tablespoons salad oil, 1 tablespoon all-purpose flour, 1 tablespoon sugar, 1 teaspoon instant minced onion, ½ teaspoon garlic salt, ½ teaspoon prepared mustard, and dash pepper. Add ½ cup water and ¼ cup vinegar; cook over medium heat to boiling, stirring constantly.

Layer the following in the hot sauce: 2 cups fully-cooked ham cut in thin strips; 3 hard-cooked eggs, sliced; ½ cup sliced celery; 3 cups torn lettuce (½ medium head); ½ cup thinly sliced cucumber; 4 ounces natural Cheddar cheese, cut in strips (1 cup); and 1 large tomato, cut in thin wedges.

Cook, covered, over medium heat 4 to 5 minutes, or till heated through. Remove from heat; toss mixture together lightly. Serve immediately. Makes 4 to 6 servings.

FIESTA SALAD BOWL

An imaginative combination for the corned beef and cabbage lover—

Cook ½ of 7-ounce package (1 cup) elbow macaroni and one 10-ounce package frozen Brussels sprouts in separate saucepans following package directions; drain. Halve Brussels sprouts. Combine cooked macaroni; halved Brussels sprouts; one 4-ounce package cooked corned beef, cut in julienne strips; 2 tablespoons chopped onion; and 2 tablespoons chopped green pepper.

Gradually stir 2 tablespoons vinegar into ½ cup mayonnaise or salad dressing. Add 1 tablespoon sugar, ½ teaspoon salt, and ½ teaspoon prepared horseradish. Pour mayonnaise mixture over macaroni mixture; toss lightly. Chill. Makes 5 or 6 servings.

BEAN AND TONGUE SALAD

Combine one 16-ounce can kidney beans, drained; 1 cup cooked tongue cut in julienne strips; ½ cup chopped celery; ¼ cup chopped candied dill pickle; 2 tablespoons chopped green pepper; and 2 tablespoons chopped canned pimiento. Blend together ½ cup mayonnaise or salad dressing, ½ teaspoon salt, and dash pepper. Toss mayonnaise with tongue mixture; chill. Makes 4 servings.

 # MENU

Bean and Tongue Salad
Poppy Seed Rolls   Butter
Hot Baked Apples with Cream
Beverage

CRAB-WILD RICE SALAD

A salad with gourmet elegance—

- 1 6-ounce package long-grain and wild rice mix
- 1 7½-ounce can crab meat, drained, flaked, and cartilage removed
- 1 tablespoon lemon juice
- ¼ cup chopped green pepper
- ¼ cup chopped canned pimiento
- 2 tablespoons snipped parsley
- ½ cup mayonnaise or salad dressing
- 2 tablespoons Russian salad dressing
- ½ teaspoon salt
- 2 medium avocados, peeled and sliced*

Cook rice following package directions; cool. Mix together crab meat and lemon juice. Combine rice, crab, green pepper, pimiento, and parsley. Blend together mayonnaise, Russian salad dressing, and salt. Add mayonnaise mixture to vegetable-crab mixture and toss lightly. Chill. Serve with avocado slices. Makes 4 or 5 servings.

*To keep avocado slices bright, dip in lemon juice mixed with a little water.

FISH SLAW

- 1 pound frozen halibut fillets, thawed
- ¾ cup mayonnaise or salad dressing
- 2 tablespoons chopped sweet pickle
- 2 tablespoons chopped onion
- 1 tablespoon vinegar
- 2 cups shredded cabbage, chilled

Place fillets in 1 quart boiling water with 1 tablespoon salt. Simmer, covered, 10 minutes, or till fish flakes easily with fork; drain. Remove skin and bones; flake fish. Combine fish with next 4 ingredients and 1 teaspoon salt. Chill 1 hour. Add cabbage; toss lightly. Sprinkle with paprika, if desired. Makes 6 servings.

CHICKEN SALAD PIE

A richly frosted salad pie—

- 1 cup sifted all-purpose flour
- ⅓ cup shortening
- ⅓ cup shredded sharp process American cheese
- 1½ cups cubed cooked chicken
- 1 8¾-ounce can pineapple tidbits, drained (⅔ cup)
- ½ cup sliced celery
- ½ cup chopped walnuts
- ¾ cup dairy sour cream
- ½ cup mayonnaise

Sift flour and ¼ teaspoon salt together; cut in shortening and ¼ *cup* cheese till pieces are size of small peas. Sprinkle 3 to 4 tablespoons cold water over, 1 tablespoon at a time, gently tossing with fork till all the mixture is moistened. Form into ball. Roll on lightly floured surface to ⅛ inch thickness. Fit into 8-inch pie plate. Bake in hot oven (450°) for 8 to 10 minutes. Cool.

Combine chicken, pineapple, celery, and nuts. Blend together sour cream and mayonnaise. Add ⅔ *cup* sour cream mixture to chicken mixture; mix well. Spoon into pastry shell. Spread remaining sour cream mixture over. Sprinkle with remaining cheese. Chill. Trim with sliced pitted ripe olives, if desired. Makes 6 servings.

LOW-CAL SCALLOP SALAD

1½ pounds frozen scallops, thawed
1 10-ounce package frozen green
   beans, cooked and drained
1 cup sliced celery
2 tablespoons chopped green onion
2 tablespoons chopped green
   pepper
2 tablespoons chopped
   canned pimiento
½ cup vinegar
1 tablespoon salad oil
   Non-caloric liquid sweetener
      equal to 1 tablespoon sugar
¼ teaspoon dried tarragon leaves,
   crushed

Place scallops and 2 tablespoons salt in 1 quart boiling water. Cover; return to boiling. Reduce heat; simmer 3 to 4 minutes. Drain and cool; slice. Combine scallops and next 5 ingredients. In screw-top jar, combine vinegar, salad oil, liquid sweetener, ¼ teaspoon salt, tarragon, and dash pepper. Cover and shake. Pour vinegar mixture over scallop mixture. Cover; chill at least 1 hour, stirring occasionally. Drain before serving. Spoon into lettuce cups. Makes 6 servings.

❧ MENU ❧

Tomato Juice
Low-cal Scallop Salad
Saltine Crackers
Fresh Blueberries   Dessert Topping
Skim Milk

BEEF 'N MUSHROOM SALAD

Also doubles as an appetizer—

Combine 4 cups cooked beef cut in julienne strips, 1 cup sliced fresh mushrooms, and ¼ cup thinly sliced green onion. Blend together ½ cup mayonnaise or salad dressing, ½ cup dairy sour cream, 1 tablespoon milk, ½ teaspoon salt, and dash pepper; toss with meat mixture. Chill. Serve in lettuce cups; sprinkle with paprika. Makes 5 or 6 servings.

TURKEY-POTATO SALAD

2 cups cubed cooked turkey
2 cups cubed, peeled,
   cooked potatoes
1 cup diced celery
4 hard-cooked eggs, coarsely
   chopped
2 tablespoons finely chopped
   onion
1 cup mayonnaise
1 tablespoon vinegar
1 teaspoon prepared horseradish
¼ teaspoon dried rosemary leaves,
   crushed

Combine first 5 ingredients. Blend together mayonnaise, vinegar, 1 teaspoon salt, horseradish, rosemary, and dash white pepper. Toss mayonnaise mixture lightly with potato mixture. Cover and chill. Serves 6 to 8.

CHEF'S SUPPER BOWL

4 cups cubed, peeled,
   cooked potatoes
1 cup sliced celery
½ cup chopped onion
½ cup Caraway Cheese Dressing
½ cup mayonnaise
½ cup chopped dill pickle
4 cups shredded lettuce
2 medium tomatoes, cut in wedges
4 slices (4 ounces) bologna,
   cut in thin strips
2 slices process American cheese,
   cut in thin strips
2 slices process Swiss cheese,
   cut in thin strips

Sprinkle potatoes with ½ teaspoon salt. Combine potatoes, celery, and onion. Blend together Caraway Cheese Dressing, mayonnaise, and pickle. Pour *half* the dressing mixture over potato mixture; toss lightly. Cover and chill. Place shredded lettuce in bottom of large bowl. Mound potato salad in center. Arrange tomatoes, bologna, and cheeses over. Pass remaining dressing. Serves 6 to 8.

Caraway Cheese Dressing: Gradually stir 2 tablespoons vinegar into one 6-ounce can evaporated milk. Add 3 tablespoons grated Parmesan cheese, ½ teaspoon salt, and ½ teaspoon caraway seed. Makes about 1 cup.

"Two's company, but three's not a crowd" when it's three servings of Jacques' Chicken Salad. Colorful extras, such as juicy tomato slices, ripe olives, and wedges of hard-cooked egg, garnish the salad. Peppy green beans, marinated with Italian dressing, complete this elegant luncheon plate.

JACQUES' CHICKEN SALAD

  1 10-ounce package frozen French-style green beans, cooked and drained, *or* 1 16-ounce can green beans, drained
 ¼ cup Italian salad dressing
  3 large chicken breasts, cooked and chilled
 ½ cup mayonnaise
 ¼ cup whipping cream, whipped
  1 cup diced celery
  3 lettuce cups
     Mayonnaise or salad dressing
  2 teaspoons drained capers
  6 tomato slices
  6 ripe olives
  2 hard-cooked eggs, quartered

In small bowl, combine green beans and Italian salad dressing. Chill several hours, stirring occasionally. Cut 3 thin slices of meat from chicken breasts and reserve for garnish. Cube remaining chicken. Gently fold the ½ cup mayonnaise into whipped cream. Fold cubed chicken, celery, ½ teaspoon salt, and dash pepper into mayonnaise-whipped cream mixture. Chill thoroughly.

Place lettuce cups on serving platter. To assemble salads, spoon chilled chicken mixture into lettuce cups. Arrange reserved chicken slices and a dollop of mayonnaise atop salad mixture; sprinkle with drained capers. Drain green beans; arrange on platter between filled lettuce cups. Garnish with tomato slices, ripe olives, and hard-cooked egg wedges. Makes 3 servings.

APPLE AND HAM SALAD

Lend a subtle flavor variation to an apple and ham toss with blue cheese—

    3 cups sliced tart apples
    1 cup cubed fully-cooked ham
    ½ cup diced celery
    ¼ cup mayonnaise or salad
        dressing
    2 tablespoons light cream
    2 tablespoons crumbled blue
        cheese
    1 tablespoon lemon juice

Combine apple slices, cubed ham, and diced celery. Blend together mayonnaise, cream, blue cheese, and lemon juice. Toss mayonnaise mixture lightly with apple-ham mixture. If desired, garnish salad with a star of unpared apple wedges. Serves 5 or 6.

GULF SHRIMP-RICE SALAD

    12 ounces shrimp, cooked, peeled,
        and cleaned *or* 3 4½-ounce
        cans shrimp, drained
    2 cups cooked rice
    1 cup chopped celery
    ½ cup shredded carrots
    ¼ cup snipped parsley
    ¾ cup mayonnaise or
        salad dressing
    2 tablespoons French salad
        dressing
    1 tablespoon lemon juice
    ½ teaspoon salt

Cut large shrimp in half; combine with rice, celery, carrot, and parsley. Blend together remaining ingredients; toss with shrimp mixture. Chill. Makes 6 servings.

PICNIC BEAN SALAD

Easy to tote to picnic site—

Cut 4 ounces salami in thin strips (1 cup). Combine with one 16-ounce can baked beans, drained; ¼ cup chopped sweet pickles; ¼ cup mayonnaise; and 2 tablespoons finely chopped onion. Season to taste. Chill several hours. Serves 3.

HOT TUNA-MACARONI TOSS

Try a hot salad for a change—

    ½ 7-ounce package (1 cup) elbow
        macaroni
    ¼ cup Italian salad dressing
    ¾ teaspoon dry mustard
    ½ teaspoon celery seed
    ½ teaspoon salt
        Dash pepper
    1 6½- or 7-ounce can tuna,
        drained and flaked
    ½ cup diced celery
    ¼ cup chopped green pepper
    ¼ cup mayonnaise or salad
        dressing
        Green pepper rings

Cook macaroni in boiling salted water till tender following package directions; drain. In skillet, mix Italian salad dressing, mustard, celery seed, salt and pepper. Heat just to boiling. Add drained macaroni, tuna, celery, and green pepper. Toss and heat through. Stir in mayonnaise. Top with green pepper rings; serve hot. Serves 4.

 MENU

Pineapple Juice
Hot Tuna-macaroni Toss
Green Beans with Parmesan Cheese
Bread Sticks   Butter
Applesauce a la Mode

CUTTING SIZE GUIDE

Terms used in recipes refer to the size of the cut-up pieces. From largest to smallest they are as follows:
Julienne—To cut food in long, thin strips.
Cube—To cut food in pieces of uniform size and shape, such as 1 inch or ½ inch.
Dice—To cut food in small cubes of uniform shape and size.
Chop—To cut food in small pieces about the size of peas.
Mince—To cut or finely chop food into very small pieces.

PORK SALAD JAMBOREE

    1 cup cubed unpared apple
    1 tablespoon lemon juice
            . . .
    2 cups cubed cooked pork
    1 cup halved and seeded
        red grapes
    ½ cup chopped celery
    ½ cup mayonnaise
    ½ teaspoon salt

Sprinkle apple with lemon juice. Toss with remaining ingredients. Chill. Serves 4 or 5.

 MENU

Pork Salad Jamboree
Buttered Broccoli
Cloverleaf Rolls   Butter
Gingerbread with Orange Sauce
Beverage

RICE AND HAM SALAD

Includes the familiar ham and cheese blend—

    ¾ cup uncooked rice
    1½ cups water
    ¼ cup finely chopped onion
    2 tablespoons soy sauce
    1 medium clove garlic, minced
            . . .
    2 cups diced fully-cooked ham
    ½ cup chopped celery
    ½ cup mayonnaise or salad
        dressing
    1 tablespoon vinegar
    ⅛ teaspoon cayenne
    4 ounces process Swiss cheese,
        shredded (1 cup)

In skillet, cook rice over low heat till lightly browned. Add water, onion, soy sauce, and garlic; mix well. Cover; cook 20 minutes or till rice is tender and liquid is absorbed. Add ham and celery; heat through. Stir in mayonnaise, vinegar, cayenne, and cheese. To serve, top with additional Swiss cheese, if desired. Makes 4 to 6 servings.

BASIC CHICKEN SALAD

    3 cups cubed cooked chicken
    1 cup chopped celery
    ¼ cup chopped sweet pickle
            . . .
    ½ cup mayonnaise or salad
        dressing
    1 tablespoon lemon juice
    ½ teaspoon seasoned salt
        Dash pepper
        Pitted ripe olive slices *or*
        hard-cooked egg slices

Combine chicken, celery, and pickle. Blend together mayonnaise, lemon juice, seasoned salt, and pepper; toss lightly with chicken mixture. Chill. Serve in lettuce cups. Trim with slices of ripe olive or hard-cooked egg. Makes 4 servings.

CHICKEN-BEAN SALAD

    1 16-ounce can cut green beans,
        chilled and drained
    2 tablespoons Italian salad
        dressing
    2 cups cubed cooked chicken
    ¼ cup sliced radishes
    ¼ cup mayonnaise or salad
        dressing
    1 tablespoon lemon juice
        Whole radishes

Combine beans and Italian salad dressing; chill at least 1 hour. Add chicken, sliced radishes, mayonnaise, and lemon juice; toss lightly. Serve in lettuce cups; garnish with whole radishes. Makes 4 servings.

HOLIDAY TURKEY SALAD

    2 cups cubed cooked turkey
    1 cup sliced celery
    1 8¾-ounce can pineapple
        tidbits, drained (⅔ cup)
    ½ cup pomegranate seeds
    ½ cup mayonnaise or salad
        dressing
    ¼ cup toasted slivered almonds

Combine all ingredients; toss. Chill. Serve on lettuce-lined plates. Serves 4 or 5.

ZIPPY SHRIMP SALAD

¼ cup dairy sour cream
¼ cup chili sauce
2 teaspoons prepared horseradish
1 pound shrimp, cooked, peeled, cleaned, and coarsely chopped
1 cup chopped celery

Blend together first 3 ingredients and ¼ teaspoon salt; stir in shrimp and celery. Chill thoroughly. Makes 4 servings.

HAM AND EGG SALAD

1½ cups cubed fully-cooked ham
6 hard-cooked eggs, coarsely diced
½ cup chopped celery
½ cup chopped sweet pickle
⅓ cup mayonnaise or salad dressing
2 tablespoons prepared mustard

Combine first 4 ingredients. Blend together mayonnaise and mustard. Add to ham mixture; toss lightly. Chill. Makes 4 servings.

TURKEY-MUSHROOM SALAD

2½ cups cubed cooked turkey
1½ cups sliced fresh mushrooms
1 cup chopped celery
2 tablespoons sliced pimiento-stuffed green olives
⅓ cup mayonnaise or salad dressing
1 tablespoon lemon juice
1 teaspoon finely chopped onion
Romaine leaves

Combine first 4 ingredients. Blend together mayonnaise, lemon juice, onion, and ½ teaspoon salt. Add to turkey mixture; toss lightly. Chill. Line salad bowl with romaine. Spoon in turkey salad. Makes 6 servings.

←**Fresh mushrooms** give Turkey-mushroom Salad a sophisticated touch. Use canned sliced mushrooms if the fresh are not available. Fill in with pert pimiento-stuffed olive slices and celery.

ALADDIN'S SALAD BOWL

4 cups torn lettuce
2 cups torn endive
1 4-ounce package sliced jellied beef loaf, cut in strips
1 4-ounce package sliced salami, cut in strips
6 ounces sliced natural Muenster cheese, cut in strips
2 hard-cooked eggs, sliced
½ cup mayonnaise or salad dressing
¼ cup Russian salad dressing

Combine lettuce and endive in salad bowl. Arrange beef, salami, cheese, and egg slices atop greens. Season to taste with salt and pepper. Combine mayonnaise and Russian dressing. Serve with salad. Serves 4 to 6.

CURRY CHICKEN SALAD

2 cups cubed cooked chicken
¾ cup diced celery
2 tablespoons raisins
½ cup mayonnaise or salad dressing
1 tablespoon lemon juice
¼ teaspoon curry powder
¼ cup whole cashew nuts

Combine chicken, celery, and raisins in large bowl. Blend together mayonnaise, lemon juice, ¼ teaspoon salt, curry powder, and dash pepper; toss lightly with chicken mixture. Chill. Just before serving, add cashew nuts and toss. Makes 4 servings.

STEWING CHICKEN FOR SALADS

Place one 5- to 6-pound ready-to-cook stewing chicken, cut up, *or* 2 large broiler-fryer chickens, cut up, in Dutch oven with water to cover (about 2 quarts). Add 2 sprigs parsley; 4 cut-up celery branches with leaves; 1 carrot, pared and sliced; 1 small onion, cut up; 2 teaspoons salt; and ¼ teaspoon pepper. Cover; bring to boiling. Reduce heat, then cook over low heat about 2½ hours till tender. Remove meat from bones. Makes about 5 cups diced cooked chicken.

TUNA-SPINACH TOSS

A perky, eye-catching salad bright with cheese strips and onion rings—

    2 cups torn spinach
    1 cup torn lettuce
    ½ small red onion, thinly sliced
        and separated into rings
        (about ½ cup)
    1 6½- or 7-ounce can tuna,
        drained and flaked
    4 ounces Swiss cheese, cut into
        narrow 2-inch strips (about
        1 cup)
    ¼ cup olive *or* salad oil
    1 tablespoon vinegar
    1 tablespoon lemon juice
    ½ teaspoon salt
    ¼ teaspoon dried tarragon
        leaves, crushed

Toss spinach and lettuce in large bowl. Place onion rings around sides of bowl. Heap tuna in center; surround with cheese. Combine remaining ingredients and dash pepper in screw-top jar; shake. Just before serving, toss dressing mixture with salad. Serves 4.

LOBSTER-ORANGE CUPS

Delicately flavored mounds of lobster with orange sections in creamy dressing—

    1 5-ounce can lobster, drained
        and cartilage removed
    3 large oranges, peeled and
        sectioned
    2 tablespoons mayonnaise or
        salad dressing
    ¼ teaspoon grated orange peel
    2 tablespoons orange juice
    ¼ teaspoon prepared horseradish
    ½ cup whipping cream, whipped

Break lobster into ½-inch pieces; sprinkle with ¼ teaspoon salt. Toss with orange sections. Chill. To prepare dressing, combine mayonnaise, orange peel, orange juice, and horseradish. Gently fold in whipped cream. Heap chilled lobster mixture in individual lettuce-lined bowls or sherbet glasses. Pass whipped cream dressing. Top with dash of nutmeg, if desired. Makes 3 or 4 servings.

HAM AND FRUIT SALAD

Ham's good flavor is highlighted with the addition of cherries and oranges—

    2 cups cubed fully-cooked ham
    1 16-ounce can pitted dark
        sweet cherries, drained
    1 11-ounce can mandarin
        oranges, drained
    1 cup chopped celery
    ½ cup mayonnaise
    1 tablespoon milk
    1 tablespoon vinegar

Combine ham, cherries, oranges, and celery. Blend together mayonnaise, milk, vinegar, and dash pepper; toss with ham mixture. Chill thoroughly. Makes 6 servings.

TURKEY-APPLE TOSS

First-class way to use leftover turkey. A hearty salad with apples and celery—

    2 cups cubed cooked turkey
    ½ cup cubed apple
    1 tablespoon lemon juice
    ¾ cup diced celery
    2 hard-cooked eggs, chopped
    ½ cup mayonnaise
    ½ teaspoon salt
    ¼ teaspoon dried basil
        leaves, crushed
      Dash pepper
    ¼ cup toasted slivered
        almonds

Toss turkey and apple with lemon juice. Add celery and eggs. Blend together next 4 ingredients; toss lightly with turkey mixture. Chill. Before serving, fold in nuts. Serve in lettuce cups. Makes 4 servings.

THURINGER SALAD

Combine 4 ounces thuringer, cubed (about 1 cup); 2 hard-cooked eggs, chopped; ½ cup chopped celery; ¼ cup cubed natural Swiss cheese; ¼ cup sliced pitted ripe olives; and ¼ cup mayonnaise or salad dressing. Toss together lightly and thoroughly. Chill well. Makes 2 or 3 servings.

HAM AND POTATO SALAD

Meat, potatoes, vegetables—all in one salad—

2 cups cubed cooked potatoes
1 tablespoon Italian
   salad dressing

. . .

1½ cups cubed fully-cooked ham
2 hard-cooked eggs, chopped
½ cup diced unpared cucumber
¼ cup sliced radishes
¼ cup chopped celery
2 tablespoons chopped onion
2 tablespoons chopped
   green pepper
¼ teaspoon salt
⅛ teaspoon paprika
½ cup mayonnaise
   or salad dressing

Sprinkle cubed potatoes with Italian dressing. Let stand ½ hour. Add remaining ingredients to potatoes *except* mayonnaise. Chill thoroughly. Before serving, gently fold in mayonnaise. Makes 5 servings.

❦ MENU ❦

Ham and Potato Salad
Grilled Tomatoes
Brown and Serve Rolls   *Butter*
Lemon Sherbet   *Chocolate Cookies*
Beverage

TUNA-MACARONI SALAD

Cook 1 cup shell macaroni following package directions. Drain thoroughly.

In large bowl, break two 6½- or 7-ounce cans tuna, drained, into large pieces. Combine tuna with drained macaroni, 1 cup sliced celery, and ¼ cup drained pickle relish.

In another bowl, blend together ¾ cup mayonnaise or salad dressing, ¼ cup Russian salad dressing, 1 tablespoon lemon juice, ½ teaspoon salt, ⅛ teaspoon pepper, and few drops onion juice. Add to tuna mixture; toss lightly. Garnish with slices from 1 hard-cooked egg. Makes 6 servings.

Fish adds a different twist to Tuna Potato Salad. Cheese and olives are also a surprise.

TUNA-POTATO SALAD

2 medium potatoes, pared
2 tablespoons Italian salad
   dressing
1 tablespoon snipped parsley
3 cups torn lettuce (about ½
   medium head)
1 9¼-ounce can tuna, drained
   and flaked
3 hard-cooked eggs, quartered
¾ cup Swiss cheese cut in strips
½ cup sliced pitted ripe olives
¼ cup chopped onion
½ cup Italian salad dressing

Cook potatoes in small amount of water for 20 to 25 minutes, till tender. Slice into salad bowl. Sprinkle with 2 tablespoons dressing and parsley. Chill. Layer remaining ingredients on top *except* ½ cup Italian dressing. Before serving, pour dressing over salad and toss lightly. Makes 4 servings.

CHOP SUEY SALAD

Combine 1½ cups cubed cooked beef *or* pork; 1 cup chopped celery; 2 hard-cooked eggs, chopped; ¼ cup diced sweet pickle; and 2 tablespoons finely chopped onion.

Blend together ½ cup mayonnaise or salad dressing, ½ teaspoon Worcestershire sauce, and ½ teaspoon salt; toss with meat mixture. Chill thoroughly. At serving time, fold in ½ cup chow mein noodles; top with additional noodles, if desired. Makes 3 or 4 servings.

CHICKEN SALAD ORIENTAL

3 cups diced cooked chicken
1 13½-ounce can pineapple tidbits, drained (1 cup)
1 5-ounce can water chestnuts, drained and sliced
2 tablespoons sliced green onion
¾ cup dairy sour cream
1 teaspoon ground ginger
¼ cup toasted slivered almonds

Combine first 4 ingredients; chill. Blend sour cream, ginger, ½ teaspoon salt, and dash pepper; add to chicken mixture and toss lightly. Serve on crisp greens. Sprinkle with almonds. Makes 4 to 6 servings.

TOSSED TUNA SALAD

Break one 9¼-ounce can tuna, chilled and drained, into large pieces. In salad bowl, combine tuna; 3 cups torn fresh spinach *or* lettuce; one 16-ounce can bean sprouts, drained and rinsed; one 5-ounce can water chestnuts, drained and sliced; 2 tablespoons sliced green onion, separated into rings; and ½ cup Italian salad dressing. Toss lightly. Garnish with 1 medium tomato, cut in wedges. Makes 6 servings.

HAM AND TURKEY TOSS

1 small head lettuce
2 heads Bibb lettuce
½ bunch curly endive
2 cups fully-cooked ham cut in thin strips
1½ cups cooked turkey cut in thin strips
2 slices natural Swiss cheese, cut in strips
1 medium avocado, peeled and sliced
1 2-ounce can anchovy fillets, drained
Chili French Dressing (see Index)

In bowl, tear greens in bite-size pieces. Arrange remaining ingredients *except* dressing atop greens. Toss salad lightly with dressing at table. Pass additional dressing. Serves 8.

GUACAMOLE SALAD BOWL

In bowl, combine 3 cups torn lettuce (½ medium head); one 6½-, 7-, or 9¼-ounce can tuna, chilled and drained; 2 tomatoes, cut in wedges; ½ cup sliced pitted ripe olives; ¼ cup chopped green onion; and 1 cup corn chips.

Combine ½ cup mashed ripe avocado; 1 tablespoon lemon juice; ½ cup dairy sour cream; ⅓ cup salad oil; 1 clove garlic, crushed; ½ teaspoon sugar; ½ teaspoon chili powder; and ¼ teaspoon *each* salt and bottled hot pepper sauce. Beat with electric mixer or blender till smooth.

Toss lettuce-tuna mixture lightly with avocado dressing. Top with ½ cup shredded Cheddar cheese. Makes 4 servings.

CRAB LOUIS

4 Bibb lettuce cups
8 cups shredded lettuce (1 large head)
2 to 3 cups cooked crab meat *or* 2 7½-ounce cans crab meat, chilled and drained

. . .

2 large tomatoes, cut in wedges
2 hard-cooked eggs, sliced
Louis Dressing
Pitted ripe olives

Line 4 salad plates with Bibb lettuce cups. Place shredded lettuce atop cups. If necessary, remove cartilage from crab meat. Reserve claw meat; leave remainder in chunks and arrange atop lettuce.

Circle with tomato and egg. Sprinkle with salt. Top with claw meat. Pour ¼ *cup* Louis Dressing atop each salad. Top with olives. Pass remaining dressing. Serves 4.

Louis Dressing: Fold 1 cup mayonnaise or salad dressing, ¼ cup chili sauce, ¼ cup chopped green pepper, 2 tablespoons sliced green onion with tops, and 1 teaspoon lemon juice into ¼ cup whipping cream, whipped. Season to taste; chill thoroughly.

An international dinner salad—Crab Louis. ➜ Chunks of crab meat, tomato wedges, and hard-cooked egg slices bask in the matchless Louis Dressing. Offer breadsticks on the side.

MOLDED MAIN DISH SALADS

SALMON AVOCADO MOLD

In saucepan, soften 1 envelope (1 tablespoon) unflavored gelatin in 1 cup cold water. Stir over low heat until all gelatin is completely dissolved.

Add 2 tablespoons sugar, 1 tablespoon lemon juice, 1 tablespoon vinegar, 2 teaspoons grated onion, ½ teaspoon salt, and ½ teaspoon prepared horseradish. Chill till gelatin mixture is partially set.

Fold in one 16-ounce can salmon, drained, flaked, and small bones removed; ½ cup mayonnaise or salad dressing; ⅓ cup sliced pitted ripe olives; and ¼ cup finely chopped celery. Spoon into 3½-cup mold; chill till gelatin mixture is firm.

To prepare avocado dressing, peel and mash 1 large avocado. Blend together mashed avocado (about ⅔ cup), ½ cup dairy sour cream, and ½ teaspoon salt. Chill. Unmold salmon salad onto serving platter; spread avocado dressing mixture evenly over outside of salad. Garnish with curly endive and a lemon twist. Makes 4 servings.

```
❧      MENU      ❧

Salmon Avocado Mold
   Sliced Tomatoes
Hard Rolls      Butter
Lemon-filled Jelly Roll
     Beverage
```

← **A spectacular salad for a foursome** is the Salmon Avocado Mold. Frosted with an avocado dressing, cut wedges are pretty on the plates. It's a do-ahead beauty to make the hostess' job easier.

CORNED BEEF LOAF

Flavorful corned beef in a delicate pink mold—

  2 envelopes (2 tablespoons)
    unflavored gelatin
  2 cups tomato juice
  1 cup mayonnaise or salad
    dressing
  2 teaspoons lemon juice
  ½ teaspoon salt
        • • •
  1 12-ounce can corned beef,
    crumbled (2 cups)
  ½ cup chopped celery
  ½ cup chopped unpared cucumber
  1 tablespoon chopped onion

In saucepan, soften gelatin in *1 cup* tomato juice; stir over low heat till gelatin is dissolved. Add remaining tomato juice, mayonnaise, lemon juice, and salt; beat smooth with rotary beater. Chill till partially set. Fold in corned beef, celery, cucumber, and onion. Pour into 8½x4½x2½-inch loaf dish; chill till firm. Makes 4 to 6 servings.

TUNA MOUSSE SQUARES

In saucepan, soften 2 envelopes (2 tablespoons) unflavored gelatin in 1½ cups cold chicken broth; stir over low heat till gelatin is dissolved. Cool. With rotary beater, beat 1 cup mayonnaise or salad dressing into gelatin mixture. Chill till partially set.

Fold in two 6½- or 7-ounce cans tuna, drained and flaked; ½ cup diced celery; 2 tablespoons chopped pimiento-stuffed green olives; 1 tablespoon finely chopped onion; 1 tablespoon lemon juice; 1 teaspoon prepared horseradish; and ¼ teaspoon paprika.

Fold in ½ cup whipping cream, whipped. Pour into 10x6x1½-inch dish. Chill till firm. Cut into squares; serve on lettuce-lined salad plates. Makes 6 servings.

SHRIMP RING SMOOTHY

A pleasing pastel gel—

2 envelopes (2 tablespoons)
   unflavored gelatin
2 cups cold water
2 cups dairy sour cream
1/4 cup catsup
2 tablespoons lemon juice
1 tablespoon prepared horseradish
1 teaspoon salt
1 pound shrimp, cooked, cleaned,
   and cut up
1 cup chopped celery
1/4 cup chopped green pepper

In saucepan, soften gelatin in cold water. Stir over low heat till gelatin is dissolved; cool slightly. Blend together sour cream, catsup, lemon juice, horseradish, and salt; add to dissolved gelatin and beat with rotary beater till smooth. Chill gelatin mixture till partially set; fold in shrimp, celery, and green pepper. Pour into 6½-cup ring mold. Chill till firm. Makes 6 servings.

Ham slices surround Potato Salad Loaf. Luncheon meat cornucopias dress up the platter.

TUNA GUMBO MOLD

1 3-ounce package lemon-flavored
   gelatin
1 cup boiling water
½ cup mayonnaise or salad
   dressing
1 10½-ounce can condensed
   chicken gumbo soup
1 6½- or 7-ounce can tuna,
   drained and flaked
½ cup chopped celery
1 tablespoon minced onion

Dissolve gelatin in boiling water; cool. Beat in mayonnaise with rotary beater till smooth; stir in soup. Chill till partially set. Fold in tuna, celery, and onion. Pour into 4½-cup mold. Chill till firm. Serves 4.

POTATO SALAD LOAF

1 8-ounce package sliced chopped
   ham (8 slices)
1 envelope (1 tablespoon)
   unflavored gelatin
½ cup cold water
1 cup mayonnaise or salad
   dressing
1/4 cup chopped celery
2 tablespoons chopped onion
1 tablespoon snipped parsley
1 tablespoon chopped canned
   pimiento
1 teaspoon prepared mustard
1 teaspoon salt
6 cups diced, peeled, cooked
   potatoes
1 8-ounce package pickle and
   pimiento loaf, diced

Line 9x5x3-inch loaf pan with waxed paper, extending paper up over sides. Line bottom and sides of pan with slices of chopped ham. In saucepan, soften gelatin in cold water; stir over low heat till dissolved; cool.

Combine mayonnaise, celery, onion, parsley, pimiento, mustard, and salt. Stir in dissolved gelatin. Fold in potatoes and diced pickle and pimiento loaf. Spoon evenly into ham-lined pan; press down lightly. Chill till firm. Unmold onto platter; remove paper. Garnish with luncheon meat cornucopias, if desired. Makes 6 to 8 servings.

PARTY HAM RING

1 envelope (1 tablespoon)
   unflavored gelatin
1 cup dairy sour cream
½ cup mayonnaise or salad
   dressing
2 tablespoons white vinegar
¼ teaspoon salt
1½ cups diced fully-cooked ham
1 cup sliced celery
2 tablespoons chopped green onion

In saucepan, soften gelatin in 1 cup cold water; stir over low heat till gelatin is dissolved. Cool slightly. Beat in sour cream, mayonnaise, vinegar, and salt with rotary beater till smooth. Chill till partially set; then whip till fluffy. Fold in remaining ingredients. Pour into 5½-cup ring mold. Chill till firm. Makes 4 or 5 servings.

HAM AND POTATO SQUARES

1½ cups diced fully-cooked ham
¼ cup chili sauce
1 tablespoon finely chopped onion
2 teaspoons prepared mustard
1 teaspoon prepared horseradish
1 envelope (1 tablespoon)
   unflavored gelatin
1 cup mayonnaise
2 cups diced, peeled, cooked
   potatoes
½ cup diced celery
2 tablespoons finely chopped
   green pepper
1 tablespoon finely chopped onion
2 teaspoons vinegar
1 teaspoon salt

Combine first 5 ingredients. In saucepan, soften gelatin in ½ cup cold water; stir over low heat till gelatin is dissolved. Stir gelatin mixture into mayonnaise; fold *half* the gelatin mixture into ham mixture. Pour into 10x6x1½-inch dish; chill till *almost* firm. Keep remaining gelatin-mayonnaise mixture at room temperature.

Combine potatoes, celery, green pepper, onion, vinegar, salt, and ⅛ teaspoon pepper. Fold remaining gelatin-mayonnaise mixture into potato mixture. Spoon over ham layer; chill till firm. Makes 8 to 10 servings.

SNOWY CHICKEN SALAD

The gelatin mixture doubles as the dressing—

2 envelopes (2 tablespoons)
   unflavored gelatin
½ cup cold water
1 13¾-ounce can chicken broth
2½ cups cubed cooked chicken
1 cup mayonnaise or salad
   dressing
½ cup diced celery
¼ cup diced green pepper
3 tablespoons sliced pimiento-
   stuffed green olives
2 tablespoons lemon juice
1 cup whipping cream, whipped

In saucepan, soften gelatin in cold water. Stir over low heat till gelatin is dissolved. Stir in chicken broth. Chill gelatin mixture till partially set.

Fold in chicken, mayonnaise, celery, green pepper, olives, and lemon juice. Fold in whipped cream. Pour into 6½-cup mold. Chill till firm. Makes 6 servings.

Two favorites come together in a superb meal-in-one salad—Ham and Potato Squares.

SEAFOOD SOUFFLE PIE

    1 stick piecrust mix
    2 3-ounce packages lime-flavored
       gelatin
    1 cup mayonnaise or salad
       dressing
    2 tablespoons lemon juice
1½ cups diced, cleaned, peeled,
       cooked shrimp
    2 cups diced avocado
   ½ cup diced celery
    2 tablespoons finely chopped
       onion

Using piecrust mix, prepare and bake one 9-inch pastry shell following package directions. Dissolve gelatin and ½ teaspoon salt in 2 cups boiling water. Stir in 1 cup cold water, mayonnaise, and lemon juice; beat till smooth. Chill till partially set. Whip till fluffy. Fold in remaining ingredients. Chill till mixture mounds when spooned. Pour into baked pastry shell. Chill 4 or 5 hours or till firm. Garnish with additional cooked shrimp, if desired. Makes 6 servings.

HAM SALAD SUPREME

    2 3-ounce packages lemon-flavored
       gelatin
   ½ cup dairy sour cream
1½ teaspoons prepared horseradish
1½ teaspoons prepared mustard
    2 3-ounce packages smoked sliced
       ham, snipped
   ½ cup diced celery

Dissolve gelatin in 2 cups boiling water. Stir in 1 cup cold water. To ½ *cup* gelatin, add next 3 ingredients and ¼ teaspoon salt; beat just till smooth with rotary beater. Pour into 5½-cup mold. Chill till *almost* firm.

    Meanwhile, chill remaining gelatin till partially set. Fold in ham and celery. Carefully pour over almost firm sour cream layer. Chill till firm. Makes 5 servings.

← **Leaf lettuce and meat flowers** spruce up Ham Salad Supreme. To make flowers, gather each ham slice at center. Secure at gathered point with halved wooden pick. Turn back outside edge.

TURKEY LIME MOLD

    2 3-ounce packages lime-flavored
       gelatin
    1 7-ounce bottle (about 1 cup)
       ginger ale, chilled
    2 cups diced cooked turkey

       • • •

    1 cup dairy sour cream
   ¼ teaspoon ground ginger
    1 16-ounce can pears, drained and
       diced

Dissolve gelatin and ¼ teaspoon salt in 2 cups boiling water; cool. To *half* the gelatin mixture, slowly add ginger ale and ½ cup cold water. Chill till partially set. Fold in turkey. Pour gelatin mixture into 6½-cup mold; chill till *almost* firm.

    Meanwhile, beat sour cream and ginger into remaining gelatin till smooth. Chill till partially set. Fold in pears. Pour over almost firm layer. Chill till firm. Serves 4.

MENU

Apple Cider
Turkey Lime Mold
Popovers   *Whipped Butter*
Hot Fudge Sundaes   *Nut Topping*
Beverage

HAM AND PINEAPPLE MOLD

    2 3-ounce packages lemon-flavored
       gelatin
    1 13½-ounce can pineapple tidbits
   ¼ cup salad oil

       • • •

    2 cups chopped fully-cooked ham
    1 cup finely shredded cabbage
   ¼ cup chopped green pepper

Dissolve gelatin in 2 cups boiling water. Drain pineapple, reserving syrup. Add enough water to syrup to make 1 cup; stir into gelatin mixture. Add salad oil. Chill till partially set. Fold in pineapple tidbits and remaining ingredients. Pour into 7½-cup mold; chill till firm. Makes 6 servings.

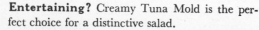
Enchant guests with crunchy Ham-cabbage Molds. They're sure to ask for the recipe.

Entertaining? Creamy Tuna Mold is the perfect choice for a distinctive salad.

HAM-CABBAGE MOLDS

Arrange with ham slices and deviled eggs—

 1 3-ounce package lemon-
   flavored gelatin
 ½ teaspoon salt
 1 cup boiling water
 ½ cup cold water
 1½ tablespoons vinegar
 ¾ cup mayonnaise or salad
   dressing
 1 teaspoon prepared mustard
 • • •
 1½ cups finely diced fully-
   cooked ham
 1 cup finely shredded cabbage
 2 tablespoons minced onion

Dissolve gelatin and salt in boiling water. Stir in cold water and vinegar. Cool mixture to room temperature. Blend in mayonnaise and mustard. Chill till partially set. Fold in ham, shredded cabbage, and onion. Pour into 5 or 6 custard cups or individual molds. Chill till firm. Unmold on lettuce-lined plates. Makes 5 or 6 servings.

CREAMY TUNA MOLD

 1 envelope (1 tablespoon)
   unflavored gelatin
 ¼ cup cold water
 2 6½- or 7-ounce cans tuna,
   drained and flaked
 ½ cup mayonnaise or salad
   dressing
 2 tablespoons lemon juice
 2 tablespoons finely chopped
   onion
 1 cup dairy sour cream
 2 tablespoons drained capers
   Unpared cucumber slices
   Cherry tomatoes

In small saucepan, soften gelatin in cold water; stir over low heat till gelatin is dissolved. In small bowl, combine tuna, mayonnaise, lemon juice, and finely chopped onion; beat till smooth. Blend in dissolved gelatin, sour cream, and capers. Spoon into 3½-cup mold; chill till firm. Unmold on lettuce-lined platter; garnish with cucumber slices and cherry tomatoes. Makes 4 or 5 servings.

SALMON FRUIT MOLD

An unusual but tasty combination—

- 2 envelopes (2 tablespoons)
  unflavored gelatin
- 2 tablespoons sugar
- ¼ cup lemon juice
- 1 cup mayonnaise or salad
  dressing
- 1 cup dairy sour cream
- 1 7¾-ounce can salmon, drained,
  flaked, and bones removed
- 1 8¾-ounce can undrained
  crushed pineapple
- 1 medium banana, thinly
  sliced (1 cup)
- ¾ cup chopped celery

In saucepan, soften gelatin in 1 cup cold water; stir in sugar. Stir over low heat till gelatin and sugar are dissolved. Cool. Add lemon juice. Combine mayonnaise and sour cream; beat into cooled mixture till smooth. Fold in remaining ingredients. Pour into 5½-cup mold; chill till firm. Makes 8 to 10 servings.

 **MENU**

Salmon Fruit Mold

Cheese-stuffed Celery   Deviled Eggs

Brioche   Butter Curls

Baked Alaska

Beverage

CURRIED CHICKEN SALAD

In saucepan, soften 2 envelopes (2 tablespoons) unflavored gelatin in 1½ cups cold water; stir over low heat till gelatin is dissolved. Remove from heat. Blend in one 10½-ounce can *condensed* chicken broth, 1 cup mayonnaise or salad dressing, 2 tablespoons lemon juice, 2 tablespoons chopped onion, and 1½ to 2 teaspoons curry powder. Beat till smooth. Chill till partially set.

Fold 2 cups diced cooked chicken and 1 cup diced celery into partially set gelatin mixture. Pour into 9x9x2-inch dish. Chill till firm. Cut into squares to serve. Serves 9.

CHEF'S MOLD

A popular salad combination made in a mold—

Dissolve one 3-ounce package lime-flavored gelatin in 1 cup boiling water; stir in ¾ cup cold water and 2 tablespoons lemon juice. Chill till partially set.

Fold in 1 cup finely shredded lettuce; ½ cup cubed fully-cooked ham; 2 ounces sharp process American cheese cut in julienne strips (½ cup); 2 tablespoons thinly sliced radishes; and 2 teaspoons finely chopped onion. Pour gelatin mixture into 3½-cup mold. Chill till firm. Unmold onto lettuce-lined platter. Makes 3 or 4 servings.

BEEF-MACARONI MOLD

- 2 3-ounce packages lemon-
  flavored gelatin
- 2 tablespoons vinegar
- ¾ cup mayonnaise
- 1 cup uncooked elbow macaroni
- 1 12-ounce can corned beef,
  flaked
- ½ cup diced celery
- 2 tablespoons chopped onion

Dissolve gelatin in 2 cups boiling water; stir in 1 cup cold water and vinegar. Add mayonnaise; beat with rotary beater till smooth. Chill till partially set. Meanwhile, cook macaroni following package directions; drain. Fold drained macaroni, corned beef, celery, and onion into gelatin mixture. Pour into 7½-cup mold. Chill till firm. Serves 8.

LOBSTER RING MOLD

In saucepan, soften 1 envelope (1 tablespoon) unflavored gelatin in ¾ cup cold milk; stir over low heat till gelatin is completely dissolved. Cool.

Beat in 1 cup dairy sour cream, 2 tablespoons tarragon vinegar, ½ teaspoon onion salt, and ¼ teaspoon salt till smooth. Chill till partially set. Fold in one 5-ounce can lobster, drained, flaked, and cartilage removed; one 8-ounce carton cream-style cottage cheese; ½ cup diced pared cucumber; and ⅓ cup sliced celery. Pour into 4½-cup ring mold. Chill till firm. Serves 4.

MORE MAIN DISHES

HOT EGG SALAD DELUXE

Prepare 1½ cups finely crushed saltine cracker crumbs. Blend together *1 cup* of the crumbs; 6 hard-cooked eggs, chopped; 1 cup mayonnaise or salad dressing; 3 slices bacon, crisp-cooked and crumbled; ½ cup diced celery; 2 tablespoons diced canned pimiento; ¼ cup milk; ¼ teaspoon salt; and dash pepper. Turn into 9-inch pie plate. Blend remaining cracker crumbs with 2 tablespoons butter or margarine, melted; sprinkle over casserole. Bake at 400° about 25 minutes, or till golden. Makes 4 servings.

SHRIMP RICE SALAD

    6 large tomatoes
    2 cups cleaned, peeled, cooked
        shrimp, cut up
 1½ cups cooked rice
    ⅓ cup chopped celery
    ¼ cup sliced pitted ripe olives
    1 tablespoon snipped parsley
    ¼ cup salad oil
    2 tablespoons red wine vinegar
    1 small clove garlic, minced
    ¼ teaspoon dry mustard
    ¼ teaspoon paprika

With stem ends down, cut tomatoes into 6 wedges, *cutting to, but not through*, bases. Spread wedges apart slightly. Carefully scoop out pulp; dice and drain pulp. Chill tomato shells. Combine diced tomato, shrimp, rice, celery, olives, and parsley.

Blend together remaining ingredients and ½ teaspoon salt; toss with shrimp mixture. Season with salt and pepper to taste. Chill. Just before serving, spoon shrimp salad into shells. If desired, trim with watercress and additional shrimp. Makes 6 servings.

← **Tomato stars,** brim full of a shrimp salad special, will highlight that springtime luncheon. Shrimp Rice Salad can be prepared in advance then spooned into the tomato shells just before serving.

QUICK TUNA SALAD

    1 16-ounce can (2 cups) macaroni
        and cheese
    1 6½- or 7-ounce can tuna,
        drained and flaked
    1 8-ounce can peas, drained
    ⅓ cup mayonnaise or salad
        dressing
    2 hard-cooked eggs, chopped
    1 tablespoon chopped green pepper
    1 teaspoon instant minced onion
    ¼ teaspoon salt
    6 medium tomatoes

Combine first 8 ingredients and dash pepper; chill. With stem ends down, cut tomatoes into 6 wedges, *cutting to, but not through*, bases. Spread wedges apart slightly. Chill tomatoes. Season insides with salt; fill with tuna mixture. Makes 6 servings.

MACARONI-CHEESE CUPS

    ½ 7-ounce package (1 cup)
        uncooked elbow macaroni
    8 medium green peppers
    2 cups cubed fully-cooked ham
    4 ounces sharp process American
        cheese, diced (1 cup)
    ¼ cup diced sweet pickle
    2 tablespoons chopped canned
        pimiento
    2 tablespoons finely chopped
        onion
    ½ cup mayonnaise
    2 teaspoons prepared mustard

Cook macaroni following package directions; drain and cool. Cut off pepper tops; remove seeds and membrane. Cook peppers in boiling salted water 5 minutes; plunge immediately in cold water. Combine macaroni, ham, cheese, pickle, pimiento, and onion.

Blend together mayonnaise, mustard, and ¼ teaspoon salt; toss lightly with macaroni mixture. Season inside of peppers with salt; fill with macaroni mixture. Chill. Serve on lettuce-lined plates. Makes 8 servings.

SALMON-FILLED TOMATOES

Scoop out centers of 6 medium tomatoes. Invert and chill tomatoes. Break one 16-ounce can salmon, drained, into small chunks, removing bones and skin. Combine salmon, 1½ cups diced pared cucumber, ½ cup mayonnaise or salad dressing, 1 tablespoon chopped onion, 1 tablespoon chopped canned pimiento, ¼ teaspoon salt, and dash pepper; chill salad mixture thoroughly.

Just before serving, sprinkle insides of tomatoes with salt. Spoon chilled salmon mixture into cavities. Serve on lettuce-lined plates. Trim with cucumber slices, if desired. Makes 6 servings.

HARD-COOKED EGGS

Place eggs in saucepan and cover with cold water at least 1 inch above eggs; rapidly bring to boiling. When water boils, reduce heat at once to keep water just *below simmering*. Cover and cook eggs 15 to 20 minutes. Cool immediately in cold water to prevent yolk darkening. To shell, crack shell all over. Roll gently between palms of hands to loosen. Start to peel from large end.

EGG SALAD ACCORDIONS

    4 medium tomatoes
    6 hard-cooked eggs, chopped
 ¼ cup finely chopped celery
 ¼ cup chopped green pepper
    2 tablespoons thinly sliced green
        onion
    2 tablespoons prepared mustard
 ½ teaspoon salt
        Dash pepper
 ¼ cup mayonnaise or salad
        dressing
        Parsley sprigs

With stem ends down, cut tomatoes into 6 slices, *cutting to, but not through*, bases. Spread slices apart slightly. Chill tomatoes. Combine eggs, celery, green pepper, onion, mustard, salt, and pepper. Stir in mayonnaise; chill. Sprinkle cut surfaces of tomatoes with salt. Fill in between slices with egg mixture. Arrange on lettuce-lined plates. Garnish with parsley. Makes 4 servings.

SHRIMP COCKTAIL SALAD

    6 medium tomatoes
    1 cup mayonnaise or salad
        dressing
    2 tablespoons minced onion
    2 tablespoons prepared
        horseradish
    4 drops bottled hot pepper sauce
 1½ cups cleaned, peeled, and
        cooked shrimp

Cut thin slices off bottoms of tomatoes to make them sit flat. Scoop out centers halfway down, reserving pulp. Invert and chill.

Finely chop reserved tomato pulp; drain well. Combine ⅓ cup chopped tomato, next 4 ingredients, and dash salt; chill. Before serving, sprinkle insides of tomatoes with salt. Hook shrimp over edges. Spoon mayonnaise mixture into cavities. Serve on shredded lettuce. Makes 6 servings.

Egg Salad Accordions, served with tumblers of iced tea, tempt appetites on a sizzling summer day.

HOT FRANK-POTATO SALAD

Dress up franks and canned potatoes—

4 or 5 frankfurters (½ pound),
    cut in ½-inch slices
1 tablespoon butter or margarine
½ envelope dry onion soup mix
1 tablespoon all-purpose flour
1 tablespoon sugar
½ cup water
2 tablespoons vinegar
2 16-ounce cans sliced
    white potatoes, drained
½ cup dairy sour cream

In skillet, brown frankfurters in butter; remove from heat. Stir in soup mix, flour, sugar, and dash pepper; add water and vinegar. Return to heat; cook and stir till boiling. Reduce heat; cover and simmer gently for 10 minutes. Stir in potatoes and sour cream; heat just to boiling. Makes 6 servings.

 # MENU

Hot Frank-potato Salad
Buttered Carrots
Dill Pickles   Bread and Butter Pickles
Strawberry Shortcake
Beverage

HAM-STUFFED TOMATOES

Asparagus lends an unusual touch—

With stem ends down, cut 8 medium tomatoes into 6 wedges, *cutting to, but not through,* bases. Spread wedges apart slightly. Chill. Cook ½ cup macaroni following package directions; drain. Combine macaroni; 1½ cups cubed fully-cooked ham; ½ of 10-ounce package frozen asparagus tips, cooked and drained; and ⅓ cup chopped celery.

Blend together ½ cup mayonnaise or salad dressing, ¼ teaspoon salt, ¼ teaspoon onion salt, and ⅛ teaspoon pepper. Add mayonnaise mixture to macaroni mixture; toss lightly. Chill. Just before serving, fill tomatoes with ham mixture. Makes 8 servings.

SHRIMP IN CHEESE RING

2 3-ounce packages lime-flavored
    gelatin
2 12-ounce cartons (3 cups) large
    curd cream-style cottage
    cheese, drained
2 tablespoons mayonnaise or salad
    dressing
1 tablespoon vinegar *or* lemon
    juice
1 tablespoon chopped onion
2 teaspoons prepared horseradish
2 cups cleaned, peeled, and
    cooked shrimp
Watercress

Dissolve gelatin in 2 cups boiling water. Add 1 cup cold water. Chill till partially set; then beat with rotary beater till fluffy. Fold in cottage cheese and next 4 ingredients. Pour into 6½-cup ring mold. Chill till firm. Unmold. Fill center with shrimp and watercress. Makes 6 to 8 servings.

THOUSAND ISLAND MOLD

In saucepan, soften 1 envelope (1 tablespoon) unflavored gelatin in ⅓ cup cold water. Stir over low heat till gelatin is dissolved. Cool. Combine ¾ cup mayonnaise or salad dressing, ½ cup chili sauce, ¼ cup catsup, 1½ teaspoons Worcestershire sauce, few drops bottled hot pepper sauce, and dash salt. Stir in gelatin mixture. Chill gelatin mixture till partially set.

Fold in 2 hard-cooked eggs, sliced and quartered; ½ cup diced celery; and 2 tablespoons chopped canned pimiento. Pour into 4½-cup mold. Chill till firm. Unmold onto serving platter. Around mold alternate halved French endives *or* lettuce wedges and Stuffed Shrimp. Makes 6 servings.

Stuffed Shrimp: Cook about 2 dozen large peeled and deveined frozen shrimp following package directions. Drain and chill thoroughly. Split shrimp part way down along vein side. Meanwhile, blend together one 3-ounce package cream cheese, softened; 1 ounce blue cheese, crumbled (¼ cup); ½ teaspoon prepared mustard; and dash garlic salt. Using pastry tube, stuff shrimp in groove split along back. Roll shrimp, cheese side down, in ½ cup finely snipped parsley.

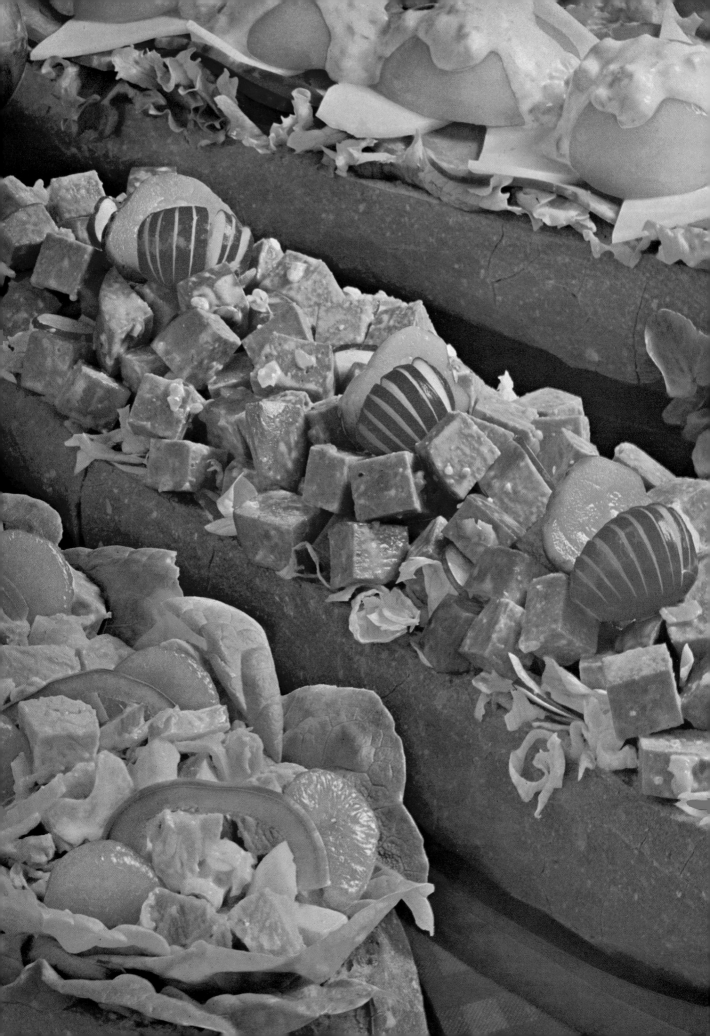

SALAD SANDWICHES

The Earl of Sandwich, originator of that world famous item, would have delighted in an opportunity to savor salad sandwiches. He might have chosen one of the many interesting and tantalizing variations found on the pages that follow.

The salad sandwich "boat" is a good example. A delicately-dressed salad nestles in the hollow of an unsliced loaf of bread which acts as the serving bowl. Fit for a king or an earl.

Or, he might have tried tempting individual salad sandwiches made by using different kinds of breads—pumpernickel, rye, or whole wheat. Rolls and English muffins also make ideal bases for meaty mixtures.

Whichever sandwich is favored, lettuce frills and decorative garnishes give it extra eye-appeal.

Prepare all three salad sandwiches—Rocky Mountain Loaf, Golden Gate Salad Loaf, and Polynesian Salad Loaf—when expecting the crowd for a buffet snack.

GOLDEN GATE SALAD LOAF

1 unsliced loaf French bread
  Butter or margarine, softened
1 ½-pound piece bologna, cut in
  ½-inch cubes (2 cups)
½ cup sliced radishes
        • • •
⅓ cup mayonnaise or salad
  dressing
¼ cup pickle relish
  Dash pepper
2 cups shredded lettuce

Cut French bread in half lengthwise; wrap top half and store for later use. Cut thin slice off bottom of remaining half to make it sit flat. Scoop out center to make slight hollow; spread inside with butter.

Combine bologna cubes and radish slices. Blend together mayonnaise, pickle relish, and pepper. Add to bologna mixture; toss lightly. Place shredded lettuce in bottom of hollow; spoon bologna mixture over. Garnish with radishes and sweet pickle slices, if desired. Makes 6 servings.

ROCKY MOUNTAIN LOAF

An electric carving knife makes serving easy—

1 unsliced loaf French bread
  Butter or margarine, softened
  Leaf lettuce
6 slices boiled ham
4 slices process Swiss cheese,
  halved diagonally
1 16-ounce can peach halves,
  well-drained
½ cup mayonnaise or salad
  dressing
2 tablespoons chili sauce
1 tablespoon pickle relish

Cut French bread in half lengthwise; wrap top half and store for later use. Cut thin slice off bottom of remaining half to make it sit flat; spread inside with butter. Arrange lettuce and ham atop bread; top with cheese triangles and peach halves.

Blend together mayonnaise, chili sauce, and pickle relish; drizzle over salad loaf. Garnish with sprigs of watercress, if desired. Makes 6 servings.

DILLY BEEF CARTWHEEL

1 cup dairy sour cream
4 teaspoons dry onion soup mix
1 tablespoon prepared horseradish
4 slices large round rye bread
1½ cups shredded lettuce
1½ cups shredded endive *or* spinach
1 medium tomato, sliced
6 thin slices roast beef
6 dill pickle strips
1 medium tomato, cut in wedges
  Milk
  Ripe olives

Combine first 3 ingredients and dash pepper. Lay 2 slices bread, bottom to bottom, to form circle; spread with ⅓ *cup* sour cream mixture. Top with *1 cup each* lettuce and endive. Place tomato slices over. Lay remaining bread atop tomato; spread with ⅓ *cup* sour cream mixture. Top with remaining lettuce and endive.

Make 6 cornucopias of beef with pickle strip in center of each; arrange with tomato wedges atop sandwich. Thin remaining sour cream mixture with a little milk; drizzle over top. Garnish with ripe olives. Cut in wedges to serve. Makes 6 servings.

AVOCADO-BACON SANDWICH

¼ cup buttermilk
½ cup mayonnaise
2 tablespoons chopped onion
½ teaspoon Worcestershire sauce
  Dash garlic salt
2 ounces blue cheese, crumbled
  (½ cup)
6 slices rye bread, toasted
  Leaf lettuce
12 slices bacon, crisp-cooked
  and drained
3 medium avocados, peeled and
  sliced
1 lemon, cut in 6 wedges

Put first 5 ingredients in blender container; add *half* the cheese. Cover and run on high speed till smooth. Stir in remaining cheese. Spread each toast slice generously with dressing. Top each with lettuce, 2 slices bacon, and avocado slices. Drizzle remaining dressing over. Garnish with lemon. Serves 6.

TUNA TUGS

Break one 6½-, 7-, or 9¼-ounce can tuna, drained, into chunks; sprinkle with 1 tablespoon lemon juice. Combine tuna; 2 hard-cooked eggs, coarsely chopped; ¼ cup thinly sliced dill pickle; 2 tablespoons thinly sliced green onion; ¼ teaspoon salt; and dash pepper. Toss lightly and chill thoroughly.

Split 3 English muffins in half; toast, then spread with softened butter or margarine. Thinly slice 3 medium tomatoes into 18 slices. Top each buttered muffin half with Boston *or* Bibb lettuce, 3 tomato slices, and tuna-egg mixture. Garnish each sandwich with dollop of mayonnaise or salad dressing. Makes 6 servings.

TURKEY SALAD-WICHES

2½ cups diced cooked turkey
¾ cup finely chopped celery
¼ cup toasted chopped almonds
2 tablespoons *each* chopped onion, chopped green pepper, and chopped canned pimiento
2 tablespoons lemon juice
⅔ cup mayonnaise
8 hard rolls, halved lengthwise

In large bowl, combine first 7 ingredients and ½ teaspoon salt. Blend in mayonnaise; chill. Scoop out center of roll halves to make slight hollow; toast. Fill each half with about ½ cup turkey mixture. Makes 8 servings.

Transform this sandwich into a low-calorie luncheon. Prepare the standard recipe for Tuna Tugs, substituting one 6½-ounce can dietetic-pack tuna for regular tuna and using 4 unbuttered toasted English muffin halves. Spoon 2 tablespoons low-calorie mayonnaise-type dressing over.

POLYNESIAN SALAD LOAF

Equally delicious served warm—

    2 cups cubed cooked chicken
    1 5-ounce can bamboo shoots,
        drained
    ½ cup sliced celery
    2 tablespoons chopped green onion
    1 hard-cooked egg, chopped
    ½ cup mayonnaise or salad
        dressing
    2 tablespoons frozen orange juice
        concentrate, thawed
    ½ teaspoon salt
    1 unsliced loaf French bread
        Butter or margarine, softened
        Bibb lettuce
        Mandarin oranges
        Green pepper slices
    ¼ cup toasted slivered almonds

Combine first 8 ingredients; chill. Cut thin slice from bottom of loaf to make it sit flat. Cut loaf in half lengthwise; wrap top half of loaf for later use.

Scoop out center of bottom half of loaf to make a slight hollow. Spread with butter. Arrange Bibb lettuce on bread. Top with chicken salad. Garnish with mandarin oranges, green pepper slices, and almonds. Serves 6.

CHEF'S SALAD IN A ROLL

    4 French rolls
        Butter or margarine, softened
        Romaine
    4 ounces sharp process American
        cheese, cut in julienne
        strips
    4 slices pressed ham
    4 slices salami
    2 hard-cooked eggs, sliced
        French salad dressing

Split rolls lengthwise, *cutting to, but not through,* crust at side. Spread cut surfaces with butter. For each sandwich, layer bottom half of roll with romaine, cheese, and ham and salami slices folded to fit roll. Place egg slices atop meat. Drizzle each sandwich with about 1 tablespoon French salad dressing. Anchor tops with wooden picks, if necessary. Makes 4 servings.

OLIVE-EGG SALAD BAKE

    1 unsliced loaf Vienna bread
    8 hard-cooked eggs,
        coarsely diced
    1 cup diced celery
    ½ cup chopped pimiento-stuffed
        green olives
    ¼ cup chopped onion
    1 clove garlic, minced
    ¼ teaspoon salt
        Dash pepper
    ½ cup mayonnaise or salad
        dressing
    2 tablespoons prepared mustard
    2 tablespoons butter or
        margarine, melted

Cut lengthwise slice from top of bread; set aside. Scoop out loaf to within 1 inch of bottom and sides. Crumble bread cut out of loaf (about 2 cups); combine with eggs and next 6 ingredients. Blend together mayonnaise and mustard; toss with egg mixture.

Spoon egg mixture into hollow loaf; replace reserved top. Brush loaf with butter; wrap in foil. Bake at 425° for 25 to 30 minutes, or till heated through. Cut loaf in 8 slices; serve immediately. Makes 8 servings.

TUNA OPEN-FACER

    1 6½-ounce can dietetic-pack
        tuna, drained
    ½ cup coarsely grated cabbage
    ¼ cup coarsely grated carrot
    1 tablespoon sliced green onion
    ⅓ cup low-calorie mayonnaise-
        type dressing
    1 tablespoon catsup
    1 tablespoon lemon juice
    ½ teaspoon seasoned salt
        Dash pepper
    4 lettuce leaves
    2 hamburger buns, split and
        toasted

LOW CALORIE · LOW CALORIE

Break tuna in chunks; combine with cabbage, carrot, and onion. Blend together low-calorie mayonnaise, catsup, lemon juice, seasoned salt, and pepper; add to tuna mixture and toss lightly. Place 1 lettuce leaf on each toasted bun half; spoon tuna salad mixture on top. Makes 4 servings.

HAM-EGG SALAD RIBBON

1 unsliced loaf white sandwich
  bread
  Butter or margarine, softened
  Ham Filling
  Egg Filling
3 3-ounce packages cream cheese,
  softened
¼ cup light cream

Trim crusts from loaf; cut in 4 equal lengthwise slices. Spread butter on one side of *three* slices. Spread remaining unbuttered slice with *half* the Ham Filling; top with second slice, buttered side down. Spread Egg Filling atop second slice; top with third slice, buttered side down. Spread remaining Ham Filling atop third slice; top with remaining bread slice, buttered side down.

Wrap loaf in foil, clear plastic wrap, or waxed paper; chill several hours. Meanwhile, beat cream cheese till smooth. Gradually add cream and beat till fluffy; frost loaf. Sprinkle with snipped parsley, if desired. Cover; chill 1 hour longer. Makes 8 to 10 servings.

Ham Filling: Combine 2½ cups ground fully-cooked ham; ½ cup mayonnaise or salad dressing; ¼ cup finely chopped celery; ¼ cup pickle relish, drained; and 1 teaspoon prepared horseradish.

Egg Filling: Combine 3 hard-cooked eggs, chopped; 2 tablespoons *each* chopped pimiento-stuffed green olives, snipped parsley, and mayonnaise; 1 teaspoon prepared mustard; and ½ teaspoon grated onion.

CORNED BEEF CAPTAINS

1 12-ounce can corned beef
4 cups finely shredded cabbage
¼ cup chopped green onion
½ cup mayonnaise
2 teaspoons prepared mustard
4 or 5 slices whole wheat bread
  Butter or margarine, softened

Chill corned beef; cut into 8 to 10 slices. Combine cabbage and onion. Blend together mayonnaise and mustard; toss lightly with cabbage mixture. Toast bread; spread with butter. Spoon cabbage mixture onto each slice; arrange 2 slices corned beef atop cabbage mixture. Makes 4 or 5 servings.

CRAB SANDWICH BROIL

Top hot apple-crab salad open-face sandwiches with a slice of melted cheese—

1 7½-ounce can crab meat,
  drained, flaked,
  and cartilage removed
½ cup chopped unpared apple
¼ cup chopped celery
½ cup mayonnaise
1 tablespoon lemon juice
3 hamburger buns, split and
  toasted
3 tablespoons butter or
  margarine, softened
6 slices sharp process American
  cheese

Combine first 5 ingredients. Spread buns with butter; top each half with ⅓ cup crab mixture. Broil 4 inches from heat for 3 to 4 minutes. Top each with slice of cheese; broil till cheese is slightly melted, about 1 to 2 minutes. Makes 6 servings.

FRANKFURTER SALAD LOAF

The "in" snack for teen get-togethers—

1 unsliced loaf French bread,
  18 to 20 inches long
4 tablespoons butter or margarine,
  softened
1 cup dairy sour cream
2 tablespoons dry onion soup mix
2 tablespoons mustard-style hot
  dog relish
4 or 5 frankfurters, thinly
  sliced (½ pound)
¾ cup chopped celery

Cut lengthwise slice from top of bread; set top aside. Scoop out loaf to within ¾ inch of bottom and sides. Spread inside of loaf and cut side of top with butter. Wrap loaf in foil, leaving cavity uncovered. Combine sour cream, onion soup mix, and relish; stir in frankfurter slices and celery. Spoon frankfurter mixture into hollow of loaf.

Bake at 375° for 25 minutes. During last 5 minutes of baking, place reserved top of loaf in oven to toast. To serve, place top on loaf; cut loaf into 1½-inch slices. Serves 12.

SALAD DRESSINGS

Salads rely on their dressings to tempt the flavor seeker beyond the first bite. Whether tart or tangy, spicy or sweet, rich or creamy—the dressing determines the success of the salad. For the simplest of recipes, salad dressings often involve little more than measuring and shaking to create gourmet fare.

Learn the difference between various types of dressings and salads which they complement best. Follow the tips for using herbs and spices to create exciting flavor variations in everyday dressings.

Look through the next few pages to inspire a new taste blend for the popular tossed salad, to discover the perfect touch for an elegant fruit salad, or to blend a hearty dressing with a favorite main dish salad.

Add tantalizing flavor to popular salads by preparing a simple Italian Dressing, a tangy Tomato Soup Dressing, or a tart and fluffy Lemonade Dressing.

CLEAR AND CREAMY DRESSINGS

FRENCH DRESSING

A top-notch basic with many variations—

- ½ cup salad oil
- 2 tablespoons vinegar
- 2 tablespoons lemon juice
- 2 teaspoons sugar
- ½ teaspoon salt
- ½ teaspoon dry mustard
- ½ teaspoon paprika
- Dash cayenne

Combine all ingredients in screw-top jar; cover and shake. Chill. Shake again just before serving. Makes ¾ cup.

Chiffonade Dressing: Prepare French Dressing adding 1 hard-cooked egg, chopped; ¼ cup chopped cooked beets; 2 tablespoons snipped parsley; and 1 tablespoon chopped onion to other ingredients. Serve with vegetable salads. Makes 1 cup.

Chili Dressing: To ½ *cup* French Dressing, add 2 tablespoons catsup, 2 teaspoons grated onion, ¾ teaspoon chili powder, and few drops bottled hot pepper sauce. Serve with vegetable salads. Makes ⅔ cup.

CREAMY FRENCH DRESSING

Combine 1 tablespoon paprika, 2 teaspoons sugar, 1 teaspoon salt, and dash cayenne. Add ⅓ cup vinegar and 1 egg; beat well. Add 1 cup salad oil in slow stream, beating constantly with electric or rotary beater till thick. Chill. Makes 1⅔ cups.

Cottage Cheese French Dressing: To 1 *cup* Creamy French Dressing, add ⅓ cup cream-style cottage cheese, 1 tablespoon chopped sweet pickle, and 1 tablespoon snipped parsley. Mix well. Serve with vegetable salads. Makes 1¼ cups dressing.

FRUIT FRENCH DRESSING

- 1 cup salad oil
- ¼ cup pineapple juice
- ¼ cup lime juice
- 1 tablespoon vinegar
- ⅓ cup sugar
- 1½ teaspoons paprika

Combine all ingredients and 1 teaspoon salt in screw-top jar; cover and shake. Chill. Shake again just before serving. Serve with fresh or canned fruit. Makes 1¾ cups.

HERB DRESSING

LOW CALORIE · LOW CALORIE

- ¾ cup wine vinegar
- Non-caloric liquid sweetener equal to 2 teaspoons sugar
- 1½ teaspoons dried basil leaves, crushed
- Dash coarsely ground black pepper

Combine all ingredients and ¼ teaspoon salt in screw-top jar; cover and shake. Chill. Shake again just before serving. Serve with meat salad bowls. Makes ¾ cup.

For salad variety, keep a selection of bottled dressings and dressing ingredients on hand.

Celery Seed Dressing with its sweet-sour balance has long been a classical accompaniment with fruit. Combine such choice fresh fruits as watermelon, pineapple, strawberries, and grapes with canned favorites. At another meal, substitute poppy seed for celery seed and serve with a vegetable salad.

CELERY SEED DRESSING

  ½ cup sugar
  ⅓ cup lemon juice
  1 teaspoon *each* celery seed, dry
      mustard, and paprika
  ¾ cup salad oil

Combine first 5 ingredients and ½ teaspoon salt. Slowly add oil, beating with electric or rotary beater till thick. Makes 1⅓ cups.

FRENCH PICKLE SAUCE

    Combine ¾ cup bottled creamy French salad dressing and ¼ cup mustard-style hot dog relish. Chill. Makes about 1 cup.

GLOSSY FRUIT DRESSING

Good with vegetable salads, too—

  ½ cup sugar
  ¼ cup vinegar
  1 teaspoon celery salt
  1 teaspoon paprika
  1 teaspoon dry mustard
  ½ teaspoon grated onion
  1 cup salad oil

In small saucepan, combine sugar and vinegar; heat and stir just till sugar is dissolved. Cool. Add next 4 ingredients and ½ teaspoon salt. Add oil in slow stream, beating with electric mixer or rotary beater till thick. Makes 1½ cups.

SNAPPY GARLIC DRESSING

The garlic is subtle—mustard adds the pep—

In screw-top jar, combine ⅔ cup salad oil; ¼ cup vinegar; 1 small clove garlic, minced; 1 teaspoon sugar; ¾ teaspoon salt; ¾ teaspoon dry mustard; and dash freshly ground black pepper. Cover and chill several hours. Shake well before serving with salad greens or shredded cabbage. Makes 1 cup.

ITALIAN DRESSING

For those who like mild seasoning—

    1 cup salad oil
    ¼ cup vinegar
    1 clove garlic, minced
    1 teaspoon salt
    ½ teaspoon white pepper
    ½ teaspoon celery salt
    ¼ teaspoon cayenne
    ¼ teaspoon dry mustard
       Dash bottled hot pepper sauce

Combine all ingredients in screw-top jar. Cover and shake well. Chill thoroughly. Shake again just before serving. Serve with vegetable salads. Makes 1¼ cups.

DRESSING DICTIONARY

French Dressing: Both clear and creamy French dressings are a mixture of oil, vinegar or lemon juice and seasonings. Clear dressings separate and must be continually shaken. Creamy dressings are homogenized and do not separate.

Mayonnaise: This creamy dressing is made by beating oil very slowly into egg, vinegar or lemon juice, and seasonings. The egg emulsifies and prevents separation.

Salad Dressing: Oil and egg are used in lower proportions than in mayonnaise. Starch pastes may be used as thickening agents and emulsifiers are sometimes added. The flavor is more tangy than mayonnaise.

Cooked Dressing: Also called boiled dressing, this type is high in egg and low in fat. It is made by cooking a white sauce-egg base to which vinegar, butter or margarine, and seasonings are added.

SESAME DRESSING

    ⅔ cup sugar
    ⅓ cup vinegar
    2 tablespoons finely chopped
       onion
    ½ teaspoon salt
    ½ teaspoon Worcestershire sauce
    ¼ teaspoon dry mustard
    ¼ teaspoon paprika
    4 to 5 drops bottled hot pepper
       sauce
    1 cup salad oil
    2 to 3 tablespoons sesame
       seed, toasted

Combine sugar and vinegar; blend in onion, salt, Worcestershire, mustard, paprika, and hot pepper sauce. Gradually add salad oil, beating constantly with rotary beater or electric mixer till thick; chill. Stir in sesame seed just before serving. Serve with fruit salads. Makes 1¾ cups.

FRENCH THOUSAND ISLAND

    ½ cup salad oil
    ¼ cup white vinegar
    ¼ cup chili sauce *or* catsup
    ½ cup evaporated milk
    2 hard-cooked eggs, chopped
    ¼ cup finely chopped green
       pepper
    2 tablespoons finely chopped
       onion
    1 small clove garlic
    ½ teaspoon salt
       Dash pepper

Combine salad oil, vinegar, and chili sauce. Gradually beat oil mixture into evaporated milk with rotary beater or electric mixer. Stir in remaining ingredients. Chill. Remove garlic before serving. Serve with tossed green salads. Makes 2 cups.

CRANBERRY DRESSING

In small bowl, beat one 8-ounce can jellied cranberry sauce till smooth. Gradually beat in ¾ cup salad oil. Blend in 3 tablespoons lemon juice and ¼ teaspoon salt. Serve with fruit salads. Makes 1¾ cups.

ZIPPY EMERALD DRESSING

    1 cup salad oil
    ⅓ cup vinegar
    ¼ cup chopped onion
    ¼ cup snipped parsley
    2 tablespoons finely chopped green
       pepper
    2 teaspoons sugar
 1½ teaspoons dry mustard
    ½ teaspoon salt
    ⅛ teaspoon cayenne

Combine all ingredients in screw-top jar. Cover; let stand at room temperature 1 hour. Shake to blend thoroughly. Serve with seafood or tossed green salads. Makes 1½ cups.

USING HERBS AND SPICES

A sprinkling of various herbs and spices gives salads distinction. Add them in small amounts, about ¼ teaspoon for four servings. Taste before adding more. For best flavor results, blend the seasonings with a little oil, then stir into the chosen dressing.

Crush dried herbs or snip fresh ones before using. If substituting fresh for dried, use 3 times more fresh herbs. Below are basic types of salads with the herbs and spices that accent them best.

Bean: oregano, savory, tarragon

Beet: chervil, dill, thyme

Coleslaw: caraway seed, celery seed, dill, poppy seed, tarragon, thyme

Cucumber: basil, chervil, dill, tarragon

Egg: caraway seed, chili powder, curry powder, dill, tarragon

Fish and Seafood: basil, celery seed, curry powder, dill, oregano, tarragon

Fruit: allspice, cinnamon, clove, ginger, mint, nutmeg, rosemary, tarragon

Meat: basil, chervil, dill, rosemary, tarragon, thyme

Potato: caraway seed, chervil, curry powder, dill, oregano, savory

Poultry: basil, curry powder, marjoram, tarragon, thyme

Tomato: basil, chervil, dill, oregano, savory, thyme

Tossed Green: basil, chervil, dill, marjoram, tarragon

Vegetable: basil, chervil, dill, oregano, savory, tarragon

TWO-WAY DRESSING

    3 tablespoons sugar
    1 teaspoon salt
    1 teaspoon dry mustard
    ¼ teaspoon white pepper
    ½ teaspoon onion juice
    ¾ cup salad oil
    ¼ cup white vinegar

For clear dressing: Combine all ingredients in screw-top jar. Cover and shake. Chill. Shake again just before serving. Serve with vegetable salads. Makes 1 cup.

For creamy dressing: In small mixer bowl, combine first 4 ingredients; add onion juice. At medium speed on electric mixer, beat in oil, a little at a time, alternately with vinegar and ending with vinegar. Makes 1 cup.

ZESTY RUSSIAN DRESSING

    1 package creamy Russian salad
       dressing mix
    ⅔ cup tomato juice
    ¼ cup vinegar
    1 tablespoon salad oil

In screw-top jar, combine all ingredients; cover and shake well. Chill. Makes 1 cup.

TOMATO SOUP DRESSING

In screw-top jar, combine one 10¾-ounce can condensed tomato soup, 1 cup vinegar, ½ cup salad oil and 1½ teaspoons Worcestershire. Add 2 tablespoons sugar, 1 tablespoon grated onion, 2 teaspoons dry mustard, 1½ teaspoons salt, ½ teaspoon paprika, ¼ teaspoon garlic powder, and dash cayenne. Cover; shake. Chill. Makes 2¼ cups.

CHILI FRENCH DRESSING

In screw-top jar, combine ⅓ cup salad oil, 2 tablespoons vinegar, 2 tablespoons catsup, 2 teaspoons grated onion, 1 teaspoon prepared mustard, ¾ teaspoon chili powder, ½ teaspoon salt, ¼ teaspoon sugar, ⅛ teaspoon dry mustard, dash pepper, dash paprika and few drops bottled hot pepper sauce. Cover and shake well. Chill. Makes about ⅔ cup.

MAYONNAISE AND COOKED DRESSINGS

LEMONADE DRESSING

1 6-ounce can lemonade
    concentrate
2 beaten eggs
⅓ cup sugar
1 cup whipping cream, whipped

Thaw concentrate. In small saucepan, combine eggs, lemonade concentrate, and sugar. Cook and stir over low heat till thickened. Cool. Fold in whipped cream. Chill. Serve with fruit salads. Makes 3 cups.

COOKED DRESSING

Combine 2 tablespoons *each* all-purpose flour and sugar, 1 teaspoon *each* salt and dry mustard, and dash cayenne in top of double boiler. Add 2 slightly beaten egg yolks and ¾ cup milk; cook and stir over *hot, not boiling,* water till thick. Stir in ¼ cup vinegar and 1½ teaspoons butter. Cool. Makes 1 cup.

MAYONNAISE

1 teaspoon salt
½ teaspoon dry mustard
¼ teaspoon paprika
    Dash cayenne

. . .

2 egg yolks
2 tablespoons vinegar
2 cups salad oil
2 tablespoons lemon juice
1 tablespoon hot water

Combine salt, dry mustard, paprika, and cayenne; blend in egg yolks. Stir in vinegar. Add oil, 1 teaspoon at a time, beating with rotary beater or electric mixer till ¼ cup has been added. Add remaining oil in increasing amounts, alternating the last ½ cup with lemon juice. Beat in water. Makes 2 cups.

RED CURRANT DRESSING

½ cup currant jelly
¼ cup mayonnaise
¼ cup whipping cream, whipped

With rotary beater, beat currant jelly till soft and smooth. Blend in mayonnaise. Fold in whipped cream. Makes about 1 cup.

BLUE CHEESE MAYONNAISE

Combine 2 tablespoons crumbled blue cheese, softened, and ½ cup mayonnaise. Beat till smooth. Stir in 4 teaspoons milk and few drops bottled hot pepper sauce. Serve with salad greens. If desired, crumble extra blue cheese over top. Makes ½ cup.

HONEY MAYONNAISE

Blend ½ cup mayonnaise, 2 tablespoons honey, 1 tablespoon lemon juice, ½ teaspoon celery seed, and ¼ teaspoon paprika. Serve with fruit salads. Makes ¾ cup.

DRESSING TIPS

French dressings—cling readily to greens and marinate vegetables. The tart-sweet ones add tang to fruit salads.

Mayonnaise and salad dressings—with their varied combinations, heighten the flavor of meat, seafood, egg, and handsome molded salads.

Cooked dressings—add luscious appeal to potato salads. Sweet cooked dressings are especially good as fruit toppings.

Cheese-flavored dressings—used with vegetables, make exciting companions.

Sour cream dressings—add zip to fruit and vegetable salads. They're delightful with main dish salad bowls.

This easy version of Thousand Island salad dressing continues as a great favorite. The creamy pink dressing is colorful with flecks of green pepper, chives, and pimiento to lend a note of cheer. Spoon it from a handsome server onto crisp lettuce wedges and garnish with sliced eggs.

THOUSAND ISLAND

> 1 cup mayonnaise
> 3 tablespoons chili sauce
> 1 tablespoon chopped green pepper
> 1 teaspoon chopped canned pimiento
> 1 teaspoon chopped chives

Blend ingredients thoroughly. Chill. Serve with lettuce wedges. Makes 1¼ cups.

FRUIT DIP FLUFF

In small saucepan, combine ½ cup sugar, ⅓ cup light corn syrup, and ¼ cup hot water. Heat slowly, stirring till sugar dissolves. Then boil without stirring to soft-ball stage (236°). Gradually beat hot syrup into 1 stiffly-beaten egg white. Add dash salt and few drops vanilla. Cool.

Fold in ½ cup mayonnaise and 1½ teaspoons shredded orange peel; chill. Serve on fruit or as a strawberry dip. Makes 1⅔ cups.

APRICOT DRESSING

Blend together ⅓ cup mayonnaise or salad dressing and ⅓ cup apricot preserves. Whip ½ cup whipping cream just till soft peaks form; gently fold into apricot mixture. Serve with fruit salads. Makes 1⅓ cups.

PARMESAN DRESSING

Combine 1 cup mayonnaise and 1 tablespoon anchovy paste. Stir in *half* envelope (1 tablespoon) Parmesan salad dressing mix, ¼ cup water, and 2 tablespoons vinegar. Serve with vegetable salads. Makes 1½ cups.

CAPER MAYONNAISE

Combine 1 cup mayonnaise, ¼ cup coarsely chopped drained capers, 3 tablespoons chopped onion, and 2 tablespoons chopped toasted almonds. Heat through; or chill. Serve with seafood salads. Makes 1½ cups.

DAIRY DRESSINGS

SWEET-SOUR DRESSING

Combine 1 cup dairy sour cream and 2 tablespoons white vinegar. Stir in 2 tablespoons sugar and 1/2 teaspoon salt. Chill. Toss with shredded cabbage. Makes 1 cup.

TARRAGON DRESSING

Combine 1 cup dairy sour cream; 1/2 cup mayonnaise; 1 teaspoon vinegar; 1/2 teaspoon dried tarragon leaves, crushed; and 1/4 teaspoon seasoned salt. Chill. Serve with seafood or vegetable salads. Makes 1 1/2 cups.

MUSHROOM DRESSING

    1 3-ounce can chopped mushrooms, drained (1/2 cup)
    1 cup dairy sour cream
    1/3 cup mayonnaise or salad dressing
    2 tablespoons well-drained pickle relish
    2 tablespoons milk
    3/4 teaspoon salt
    1/2 teaspoon Worcestershire sauce

Chop any large pieces of mushrooms. Combine with remaining ingredients; chill thoroughly. Serve with lettuce wedges or vegetable salads. Makes 2 cups.

COTTAGE CHEESE FLUFF

    1 cup cottage cheese, not creamed
      Non-caloric liquid sweetener equal to 2 tablespoons sugar
    4 teaspoons lemon juice
    1/2 cup skim milk

In blender container, combine cottage cheese, sweetener, and lemon juice; blend till creamy. Add milk, a tablespoon at a time, till of desired consistency. Serve with shredded cabbage or lettuce. Makes 1 cup.

NIPPY NECTAR DRESSING

Beat together one 3-ounce package cream cheese, softened; 2 tablespoons honey; 1 teaspoon grated lemon peel; 1 tablespoon lemon juice; and 1/8 teaspoon salt. Gradually add 1/2 cup salad oil, beating till mixture is thickened. Chill. Serve with fruit. Makes 1 cup.

CUCUMBER DRESSING

Blend together 1/2 cup finely chopped unpared cucumber, 2 tablespoons mayonnaise, 1 tablespoon lemon juice, 1/8 teaspoon salt, and 1/8 teaspoon paprika. Whip 1/2 cup whipping cream just till soft peaks form. Fold into cucumber mixture. Chill. Serve with seafood salads. Makes 1 1/4 cups.

CREAM FRENCH DRESSING

With electric mixer, blend one 3-ounce package cream cheese, softened, with 1 tablespoon milk. Stir in 1/2 teaspoon sugar, 1/2 teaspoon paprika, and 1/4 teaspoon salt. Gradually add 1 tablespoon vinegar, then 6 tablespoons salad oil, beating till fluffy. Chill. Makes 3/4 cup.

WALNUT DRESSING

Blend together 1/3 cup mayonnaise; 1/4 cup chopped walnuts; and 2 to 3 tablespoons frozen orange juice concentrate, thawed. Whip 1/2 cup whipping cream just till soft peaks form; fold into mayonnaise mixture. Chill. Serve with fruit. Makes 1 1/2 cups.

CHEF'S CHEESE DRESSING

Thoroughly combine 3 ounces blue cheese, crumbled (3/4 cup); 1/2 cup olive or salad oil; 2 tablespoons white vinegar; 1 tablespoon lemon juice; 1 teaspoon anchovy paste; and 1/2 clove garlic, minced. Season to taste. Chill. Stir before serving. Makes 1 cup.

LOW CALORIE · LOW CALORIE

Complement a pretty molded fruit salad with the mellow flavor of creamy Banana Cheese Dressing. It's a dressing good any season of the year and not limited to molded gelatin salads. Try it with a fresh fruit plate in summer, or spoon over canned or citrus fruits during winter.

BANANA-CHEESE DRESSING

Blend one 3-ounce package cream cheese, softened, with 2 tablespoons milk. Mash 1 fully-ripe banana (½ cup); add 1 tablespoon *each* sugar and lemon juice, and dash salt. Stir banana mixture into cheese mixture. Serve with fruit salads. Makes 1 cup.

BERRY SOUR CREAM SAUCE

1 cup dairy sour cream
½ 10-ounce package frozen sliced
    strawberries, thawed (½ cup)

Blend cream and fruit. Chill. Serve with fruit salads. Makes about 1¼ cups.

DAIRY FRUIT DRESSING

Combine ½ cup dairy sour cream, 1 tablespoon honey, 1 teaspoon lemon juice, and ¼ teaspoon salt. Chill. Serve with sweetened or canned fruit. Makes about ½ cup.

AVOCADO DRESSING

Sieve 1 large ripe avocado, peeled (about ¾ cup); immediately add 2 to 3 tablespoons lemon juice. Stir in ½ cup light cream, ¾ teaspoon salt, ½ teaspoon prepared mustard, and ¼ teaspoon Worcestershire sauce. Chill. Serve with shredded cabbage or lettuce wedges. Sprinkle with ¼ cup crumbled blue cheese, if desired. Makes 1 cup.

Fresh vegetable texture from cucumber, radishes, green pepper, and green onion gives Crunchy Cream Dressing its name. This sour cream dressing tops off any green salad but is especially good on lettuce or cabbage. Additional green pepper rings or cucumber twists make notable garnishes.

CRUNCHY CREAM DRESSING

- ½ cup finely chopped unpared cucumber
- 2 tablespoons finely chopped green pepper
- 2 tablespoons finely chopped green onion
- 2 tablespoons thinly sliced radishes
- 1 cup dairy sour cream
- ½ teaspoon salt
  Dash pepper

Combine cucumber, green pepper, onion, and radishes. Stir in sour cream, salt, and pepper; mix well. Chill thoroughly. Serve over lettuce or cabbage salads. Makes 1½ cups.

SPICY FRUIT DRESSING

Combine 1 cup dairy sour cream, ½ cup apple cider or apple juice, ½ cup salad oil, ½ teaspoon ground cinnamon, ¼ teaspoon ground nutmeg, and dash salt; beat with rotary beater till smooth. Chill thoroughly. Serve with fruit salads. Makes 2 cups.

MARMALADE DRESSING

Blend together ½ cup dairy sour cream, 2 tablespoons orange marmalade, 2 teaspoons lemon juice, ¼ teaspoon paprika, and dash salt. Gently fold in ½ cup whipping cream, whipped. Chill thoroughly. Serve with fruit salads. Makes about 1½ cups.

YOGURT SALAD DRESSING

1 cup plain yogurt
2 teaspoons milk
1 teaspoon lemon juice
¼ teaspoon garlic salt
¼ teaspoon onion salt
  Dash dried rosemary leaves,
    crushed

Combine all ingredients; chill. Serve with vegetable salads. Makes 1 cup.

CREAMY CHEESE DRESSING

In screw-top jar, combine ¾ cup dairy sour cream and 2 ounces blue cheese, crumbled (½ cup); stir in 2 tablespoons milk. Add 1 tablespoon salad oil, 2 teaspoons grated Parmesan cheese, and dash *each* onion salt, garlic salt, pepper, and Worcestershire sauce; mix well. Add 3 tablespoons white wine vinegar; cover jar and shake well. Chill. Serve with vegetable salads. Makes 1⅓ cups.

ROSY SALAD DRESSING

Swirling cranberry relish adds glamour—

Combine one 8-ounce package cream cheese, softened, and 1 cup dairy sour cream; beat till smooth. Stir in ¾ cup cranberry relish. Chill at least 2 hours. Serve with fruit salads. Makes about 3 cups.

AVOCADO CREAM DRESSING

Tastes as good as it sounds—

1 medium avocado, peeled and
    mashed
½ cup dairy sour cream
2 tablespoons milk
2 teaspoons lemon juice
½ teaspoon salt
¼ teaspoon dried chervil leaves,
    crushed
  Dash onion powder
3 drops bottled hot pepper sauce

Combine all ingredients; chill. Serve with tomato or lettuce wedges. Makes 1 cup.

ROQUEFORT DRESSING

½ cup mayonnaise
½ cup light cream
1½ teaspoons lemon juice
4 ounces Roquefort *or* blue cheese

Combine mayonnaise, light cream, and lemon juice. Crumble cheese into mayonnaise mixture; mix well. Chill. Serve with lettuce or tomato wedges. Makes 1½ cups.

FRENCH CHEESE DRESSING

1 3-ounce package cream cheese,
    softened
2 ounces Roquefort *or* blue
    cheese, crumbled (½ cup)
½ cup French salad dressing

Beat cream cheese and Roquefort cheese together. Stir in French dressing. Chill. If dressing thickens during refrigeration, stir in additional French salad dressing to desired consistency. Makes 1 cup.

CITRUS PEANUT DRESSING

¼ cup peanut butter
¼ teaspoon grated orange peel
¼ teaspoon prepared mustard
½ cup dairy sour cream
3 tablespoons orange juice

Combine peanut butter, orange peel, mustard, and dash salt. Gradually stir in sour cream and orange juice. Serve with fresh fruit salads. Makes about 1 cup dressing.

HORSERADISH DRESSING

½ cup dairy sour cream
¼ cup mayonnaise or salad
    dressing
1 tablespoon prepared horseradish
1 teaspoon sugar
¼ teaspoon salt
2 drops bottled hot pepper sauce
2 drops Worcestershire sauce

Combine all ingredients; chill. Serve with meat or seafood salads. Makes 2 cups.

ROBUST RELISHES

Thank the early American Colonists for many tasty relishes filled with a sweet-sour piquancy. In those days, pickles and relishes were standard fare that appeared at every meal.

The relish, often a mixture of chopped vegetables or fruits, herbs, spices, and seasonings, adds flavor and zest to the main portion of a meal. The recipes in this chapter are adaptations of this basic theme. Serve them as a side dish with the main course or in conjunction with a lavish buffet menu.

A good relish should have attractive color as well as appetizing appearance. Most, but not all, relishes are crisp and contain fairly uniform-size pieces combined with a small amount of liquid. The mixture should be moist, but never watery.

This tiered relish server invites dinner guests to help themselves to a triple treat of chilled relishes—Pickled Mushrooms, Cheese-fruit Relish, and Carrot-olive Slaw.

SUMMER CORN RELISH

Wonderful way to preserve fresh corn—

2 cups sugar
2 cups vinegar
1½ teaspoons celery seed
½ teaspoon turmeric
2 cups chopped onion
2 cups chopped tomato
2 cups chopped cucumber
2 cups corn, cut from cob
2 cups chopped cabbage

In Dutch oven, combine first 4 ingredients and 1½ teaspoons salt. Heat to boiling; add vegetables. Cook, uncovered, 25 minutes, stirring occasionally. Pack in hot, scalded jars and seal. Makes 3 pints.

A platter of Sunburst Artichoke brightens a menu. Garnish the center with sprigs of parsley.

SUNBURST ARTICHOKE

1 artichoke
1 cup mayonnaise or salad dressing
2 teaspoons dry mustard
1 teaspoon Worcestershire sauce
3 hard-cooked eggs

Cook artichoke in boiling salted water about 30 minutes; drain. Chill. Pull off leaves; trim off points. Mix mayonnaise, mustard, and Worcestershire sauce.

Halve hard-cooked eggs crosswise; cut each half into 8 wedges. Top leaves with dollop of dressing; place an egg wedge at base of leaf. Arrange sunburst-fashion on platter.

CALIFORNIA GUACAMOLE

Peel and chop 2 large avocados. Peel and chop one large tomato, removing seeds; drain. Put avocado and tomato in blender or mixer bowl; add 2 tablespoons finely chopped onion and 1 tablespoon wine vinegar. Blend or beat till smooth. Season with ½ teaspoon salt and dash pepper. Serve over tomatoes. Makes about 2 cups.

BANANA CUTS

¼ cup honey
2 teaspoons lemon *or* lime juice
3 ripe bananas
1 cup shredded coconut, toasted*

Combine honey and lemon juice. Peel bananas; cut diagonally in thirds. Brush honey mixture on bananas; roll in coconut.

*To toast coconut, spread thin layer of coconut in shallow baking pan. Toast in oven at 350° till lightly browned, about 6 to 7 minutes. (Stir coconut or shake pan often during baking to toast evenly.)

APPLE-STICK RELISH

Combine 2 unpared tart apples, chopped; ¼ cup chopped onion; and ¼ cup chopped dill pickle. Combine ¼ cup sugar and 2 tablespoons vinegar. Toss with apple mixture; chill. Makes about 3 cups.

CARROT-OLIVE SLAW

Use with Cheese-fruit Relish and Pickled Mushrooms to make a tasty relish trio—

1/4 cup salad oil
2 tablespoons vinegar
2 tablespoons sugar
1/2 teaspoon salt
3 cups shredded carrots
1/4 cup sliced pitted ripe olives

Combine salad oil, vinegar, sugar, salt, and dash pepper; toss lightly with carrots and olives. Chill. Makes 2 1/2 cups.

CHEESE-FRUIT RELISH

1 16-ounce carton (2 cups) large curd cream-style cottage cheese, drained
1 cup halved seedless green grapes
2 tablespoons coarsely chopped pistachio nuts
1/3 cup mayonnaise or salad dressing
1/4 teaspoon salt

Combine all ingredients; mix together lightly. Chill. Serve in relish dish or spoon into lettuce cup placed in the center of a fruit platter. Makes about 2 2/3 cups.

PICKLED MUSHROOMS

2/3 cup tarragon vinegar
1/2 cup salad oil
1 medium clove garlic, crushed
1 tablespoon sugar
2 tablespoons water
Dash bottled hot pepper sauce
1 medium onion
2 6-ounce cans mushroom crowns, drained

Combine vinegar, salad oil, garlic, sugar, 1 1/2 teaspoons salt, dash pepper, water, and hot pepper sauce. Slice onion and separate into rings; add to marinade along with mushrooms. Cover; refrigerate 8 hours or overnight, stirring several times. Drain before serving. Makes 2 cups.

DILLED CARROTS

1/4 cup finely chopped onion
1 tablespoon snipped parsley
1/2 cup low-calorie Italian salad dressing
1/2 teaspoon dillweed
1/4 teaspoon salt
Dash freshly ground black pepper
. . .
1 16-ounce can (2 cups) whole carrots, drained

LOW CALORIE · LOW CALORIE

Combine onion, parsley, Italian salad dressing, dillweed, salt, and pepper and pour over carrots in shallow dish. Cover; refrigerate several hours or overnight, stirring occasionally. Drain before serving. Makes 2 cups.

DEVILED GUACAMOLE

2 avocados, halved and peeled
1 2 1/4-ounce can deviled ham
2 tablespoons chopped green chilies
2 teaspoons lemon juice
1 teaspoon grated onion

Mash avocados with fork. Stir in remaining ingredients and dash salt; chill. Serve as relish or dip. Makes 1 1/2 cups.

BEAN RELISH

1 16-ounce can whole green beans
1/3 cup vinegar
2 tablespoons sugar
1 teaspoon salt
1 teaspoon dillseed
1 teaspoon mixed pickling spices
. . .
1 medium onion, sliced and separated in rings
1 tablespoon salad oil

Drain beans, reserving liquid. In saucepan, combine reserved liquid with vinegar, sugar, salt, dillseed, and mixed pickling spices; simmer 5 minutes. Add beans; heat through. Cool mixture, then drain off excess liquid. Toss beans with onion rings and salad oil. Chill before serving. Makes about 2 cups.

PEPPY BEET SALAD

Spicy and pickly—

1 16-ounce can sliced *or* diced
    beets
⅓ cup vinegar
1 tablespoon sugar
½ teaspoon ground cinnamon
¼ teaspoon ground allspice
    Dash ground cloves

• • •

¼ cup pickle relish
2 tablespoons chopped onion

Drain beets, reserving liquid. Add enough water to liquid to make 1 cup; add vinegar, sugar, cinnamon, allspice, and cloves. Bring to boiling. Stir in beets; bring to boiling again. Remove from heat. Chill beets in liquid. Drain; stir in pickle relish and onion. Mix well. Makes 2 cups.

GARLIC OLIVES

⅔ cup salad oil
⅓ cup wine vinegar
3 cloves garlic, minced
1 9-ounce can ripe olives,
    drained (about 1½ cups)

Combine salad oil, vinegar, and garlic. Pour over olives. Refrigerate several hours or overnight, stirring occasionally. Drain before serving. Makes 1½ cups.

FRESH CUCUMBER RELISH

Refreshing hint of dill—

3 medium cucumbers
½ medium onion

• • •

⅓ cup vinegar
1 tablespoon sugar
½ teaspoon salt
¼ teaspoon dried dillweed

Slice cucumbers in half lengthwise; scoop out seeds and discard. With food chopper using coarse blade, grind cucumbers and onion; drain. Stir in remaining ingredients. Chill thoroughly. Makes about 1¾ cups.

TOMATO-PEPPER RELISH

Combine 3 cups diced tomatoes, 2 cups chopped green pepper, and ¼ cup Italian salad dressing. Chill several hours, stirring occasionally. Just before serving, drain well. Makes 4 cups relish.

CONFETTI RELISH

1 16-ounce can French-style green
    beans, drained
1 12-ounce can whole kernel corn,
    drained
1 8½-ounce can peas, drained
1 6-ounce can sliced mushrooms,
    drained
¼ cup chopped onion
¼ cup diced canned pimiento
⅓ cup white wine vinegar
¼ cup sugar
1 teaspoon salt
½ cup salad oil

Combine first 6 ingredients in large bowl. In screw-top jar, combine vinegar, sugar, and salt; cover and shake till sugar is dissolved. Add oil and shake well. Pour oil mixture over vegetable mixture. Chill several hours, stirring occasionally. Drain well before serving. Makes about 5 cups.

DEVILED EGGS

6 hard-cooked eggs, halved
    lengthwise
¼ cup mayonnaise or salad
    dressing
1 tablespoon finely chopped onion
1 tablespoon finely chopped
    pimiento-stuffed green olives*
1½ teaspoons prepared mustard
⅛ teaspoon salt
    Dash pepper
    Paprika

Remove egg yolks from whites. Mash yolks and combine with next 6 ingredients. Refill egg whites, using pastry tube, if desired. Chill. To serve, sprinkle tops with paprika.

*Or, substitute crisp-cooked and crumbled bacon, chopped canned pimiento, snipped chives, sweet pickle, or snipped parsley.

CHERRY RELISH

- 1 20-ounce can pitted tart red cherries
- ½ cup raisins
- ½ cup honey
- ½ cup vinegar
- ¼ cup brown sugar
- ½ teaspoon ground cinnamon
- ⅛ teaspoon ground cloves
- ½ cup chopped pecans
- 1 tablespoon cornstarch
- 1 tablespoon cold water

In 2-quart saucepan, combine cherries, raisins, honey, vinegar, brown sugar, cinnamon, and cloves. Cook slowly, uncovered, for 30 minutes. Stir in nuts. Combine cornstarch and water; gradually stir into cherry mixture. Cook, stirring constantly, till mixture thickens and bubbles. Chill. Makes 2½ cups.

CHEESE-ONION MARINADE

A choice barbecued meat partner—

- 3 ounces blue cheese, crumbled (¾ cup)
- ½ cup salad oil
- 2 tablespoons lemon juice
- 1 teaspoon salt
- ½ teaspoon sugar
  Dash pepper
  Dash paprika

. . .

- 4 medium onions, thinly sliced and separated into rings (about 4 cups)

Mix all ingredients *except* onion rings. Pour mixture over onion rings and refrigerate at least 3 to 4 hours. Makes about 4 cups rings.

APPLESAUCE RELISH

- 1 16-ounce can applesauce
- ¼ cup red cinnamon candies
- 1 teaspoon prepared horseradish

In saucepan, combine applesauce, candies, and horseradish. Cook and stir over medium heat till candies are dissolved. Cool; refrigerate till ready to serve. Makes 2 cups.

COMBINATION RELISH

- 1 teaspoon salt
- 1 cup chopped cabbage
- ½ cup chopped carrots
- ¼ cup sugar
- 1 tablespoon dry mustard
- 1 teaspoon cornstarch
- ⅓ cup vinegar
- 1 8-ounce can whole kernel corn, drained
- ¼ teaspoon celery seed

Mix salt with cabbage; let stand 1 hour. Drain well. Cook carrots 3 to 5 minutes in small amount of boiling water; drain. In saucepan, combine sugar, mustard, and cornstarch. Blend in vinegar and ¼ cup cold water. Cook and stir over medium heat till mixture thickens and bubbles. Add cabbage carrots, corn, and celery seed. Bring to boiling; cook 5 minutes. Chill. Makes 1⅔ cups.

CELERY CRAN-RELISH

Using coarse blade of food chopper, grind 1 pound fresh cranberries; 2 cups coarsely chopped celery; and 1 medium unpared apple, cut up. Stir in 1½ cups sugar and 2 tablespoons lemon juice; chill. Keeps in refrigerator several weeks. Makes about 4 cups.

PICKLED APRICOTS

- 1 cup dried apricots
- 1 cup brown sugar
- ¼ cup vinegar
- 2 inches stick cinnamon
- 6 whole cloves
- 24 to 30 walnut halves

Rinse apricots. In saucepan, cover apricots with 1-inch water. Cover and simmer gently for 15 minutes. Drain, reserving ¾ cup apricot liquid. In saucepan, combine reserved apricot liquid, brown sugar, vinegar, stick cinnamon, and whole cloves. Stir in apricots; return to boiling and simmer, covered, 10 minutes more, or till tender.

Cool apricots in syrup. Refrigerate till ready to serve. At serving time, remove apricots from syrup. Fill each apricot half with a walnut half. Makes 2 to 2½ dozen.

BUYING, STORING, AND PREPARING

Being a successful salad maker is not difficult, but it does necessitate adequate planning. Charts, buying and storing know-how, and preparation tips can ease this job.

This final chapter comes to the rescue with all the information a homemaker needs. Becoming familiar with the how-to's of making attractive garnishes for salads is not complicated. The ones pictured at left are described on page 154.

Citrus Garnishes are an easy way to vary and flatter salad servings.

The Orange Chrysanthemum makes a beautiful centerpiece on a fruit platter.

A bouquet of Vegetable Flowers is turned out in a jiffy by using cookie cutters.

Serve mayonnaise in a Cucumber Basket to pass with a vegetable salad.

HOW MUCH AND HOW MANY

Food	Amount
Cereals	
Macaroni	4 ounces uncooked (1 to 1¼ cups) = 2¼ cups cooked
Rice, long-grain	6½ to 7 ounces uncooked (1 cup) = 3 to 4 cups cooked
packaged precooked	1 cup uncooked = 2 cups cooked
Spaghetti	7 ounces uncooked (1½ to 2 cups) = 4 cups cooked
Dairy Products	
Blue cheese, crumbled	4 ounces = 1 cup
American or Cheddar cheese, shredded or cubed	1 pound = 4 cups
Sour cream or yogurt	8 ounces = 1 cup
Whipping cream	1 cup unwhipped = about 2 cups whipped
Fresh Fruit	
Apple, chopped	1 medium = about 1 cup
Banana, sliced	1 medium = ⅓ to ½ cup
Grapes, halved and seeded	1 pound = 2 cups
Lemon, juice	1 medium = 3 tablespoons
grated peel	1 medium = 1 teaspoon
Orange, juice	1 medium = about ⅓ cup
grated peel	1 medium = about 2 teaspoons
Peach or pear, sliced	1 medium = ½ cup
Strawberries, sliced	1 quart = 4 cups
Fresh Vegetables	
Cabbage, shredded	1 medium head = 8 cups
Carrots, shredded	1 pound (without tops) = 3 cups
Celery, diced or chopped	8 branches = 2¾ cups
Green onions, sliced with tops	7 onions (1 bunch) = about ½ cup
Green pepper, diced	1 large (6 ounces) = 1 cup
Iceberg lettuce, torn in bite-size pieces	1 small head = 4 cups
	1 medium head = 6 cups
	1 large head = 8 cups
Onion, chopped	1 medium = ½ cup
Potato, cooked and cubed	4 medium = 4 cups
Radishes, sliced	1 bunch = about 1 cup
Meat and Seafood	
Chicken, cooked and diced	
Broiler-fryer	about ¾ cup per pound
Stewing chicken	about 1 cup per pound
Two chicken breasts, 10 ounces each	1½ to 2 cups diced *or* 12 thin slices
Shrimp, cleaned and cooked	2 ounces raw in shell *or* 7 or 8 ounces frozen, shelled *or* one 4½- or 5-ounce can = 1 cup

Food	Amount
Nuts Almonds Pecans or walnuts, halved or chopped	1 pound unshelled = ¾ to 1 cup shelled 1 pound unshelled = 1½ to 1¾ cups
Miscellaneous Cherries, whole candied Coconut, flaked shredded Gelatin, unflavored flavored, packaged	1 pound = 2¼ cups 3½ ounces = 1⅓ cups 4 ounces = 1⅓ cups 1 ounce = 4 tablespoons 1 envelope = 1 tablespoon 3 ounces = 7 tablespoons

COMMON CAN AND JAR SIZES

Container	Approximate Net Weight or Fluid Measure	Approximate Cups
8 ounce	8 ounces	1
Picnic	10½ to 12 ounces	1¼
12 ounce (vacuum)	12 ounces	1½
No. 300	14 to 16 ounces	1¾
No. 303	16 to 17 ounces	2
No. 2	20 ounces (18 fluid ounces)	2½
No. 3 cylinder *or* 46 fluid ounce	51 ounces (46 fluid ounces)	5¾
No. 10	6½ to 7¼ pounds	12 to 13

WEIGHTS AND MEASURES

1 dash = 1/16 teaspoon 3 teaspoons = 1 tablespoon 4 tablespoons = ¼ cup 5⅓ tablespoons = ⅓ cup 8 tablespoons = ½ cup 10⅔ tablespoons = ⅔ cup 16 tablespoons = 1 cup 1 ounce = 28.35 grams 1 pound = 453.59 grams	1 gram = 0.035 ounces 1 kilogram = 2.21 pounds 1 cup = 8 fluid ounces 2 cups = 1 pint 4 cups = 1 quart 4 quarts = 1 gallon 8 quarts = 1 peck 1 quart = 946.4 milliliters 1 liter = 1.06 quarts

GUIDE TO BUYING FRUIT

Apples: For best flavor choose those having good color for the specific variety. They should be firm to the touch. Avoid those which yield to slight pressure and are soft and mealy. Good salad apples include Delicious and Golden Delicious, sweet; Cortlands, mild; McIntosh and Winesaps, slightly tart; and Jonathans and Staymans, tart.

Apricots: Avoid apricots feeling soft or looking shriveled and wilted. Good ones appear golden-yellow, plump, and fairly firm.

Avocados: They vary in size, shape, and color from green to almost black. If ripe, they will yield to gentle pressure.

Berries: Look for berries that are firm, plump, and full-colored. They should be bright, clean, and fresh in appearance. Only strawberries should have a hull (stem cap) attached when mature.

Figs: Buy figs for immediate use since they are very perishable. Fully ripe fresh figs should be fairly soft to the touch. One with a sour odor indicates it is overripe.

Grapefruit: Pick those that are firm, well-shaped, heavy for their size, and smooth textured. The color of the skin is not always a good way to judge flavor and ripeness. Grapefruit, even though ripe, may have a green tinge. Russeted fruit often is tastier and juicier than the brightly colored fruit.

Grapes: Choose well-formed grape clusters. Color is an excellent guide to ripeness. Darker varieties should be free of green tinge, and green grapes should show a slight amber blush. When ripe, all grapes should be fairly soft and tender to the touch.

Kiwi: Kiwi fruits are imported from New Zealand. Sometimes called Chinese gooseberries, these brown fuzzy-skinned fruits will be soft to the touch, like an avocado, when ripe. To serve this fruit, peel and slice.

Lemons: Buy those that are moderately firm, fine textured, and heavy for size.

Limes: Green ones are more acid than the yellow-colored ones. Both should be heavy for their size, indicating high juice content.

Mangoes: They will vary in size from a plum to an apple and from yellow to red in coloring. The smooth skin is often speckled with black. Select those that are solid and not too soft to the touch.

Melons: Good melons show no evidence of a stem at the blossom end. Good, ripe cantaloupes have delicate aroma and a thick netting that stands out. The skin under the netting should have a yellow tinge. Ripe honeydews should have a pleasant aroma and creamy-yellow rinds. Watermelons should have dull surfaces and be symmetrical in shape. Color and aroma are the best guides to choosing melons.

Nectarines: Choose as for peaches.

Oranges: Look for oranges that are heavy for their size, firm, and with skins that are not too rough. Naval oranges are seedless, slightly thick-skinned, and are easy to peel and segment, making them good for salads. Temple oranges are very juicy, easy to peel, and have a rich flavor.

Papayas: Look for greenish-yellow to full-yellow color and flesh that will give slightly when fruit is pressed in palm of hand.

Peaches: They should be plump and fairly firm. Depending on variety, the skin color should be white or yellow with a red blush.

Pears: When ripe, they will yield to gentle pressure at the stem end. Colors range from creamy yellow to russet.

Persimmons: Choose ones that are firm and shapely, plump, and highly colored (orange-red). Handle gently because they are delicate. They resemble large ripe tomatoes in shape and firmness. Be sure stem cap is attached when buying.

Plums: Pick plums that are plump, full-colored, and soft enough to yield to slight pressure. Softening at the tip is usually a sign that the fruit is mature. Avoid those that are shriveled and hard.

Pomegranates: Those with thin skins of bright purply-red color and fresh appearance are the best ones to buy.

GUIDE TO BUYING VEGETABLES

Artichokes (globe): Choose artichokes that are heavy, compact, and have a plump globe with large, tightly-closed, fleshy leaf scales. Good green color is also important.

Asparagus: Select asparagus spears that have tightly closed buds at the top with straight, tender, and fresh-appearing stalks. There should be little tough base to trim off.

Beans: They should have crisp, long, straight, blemish-free pods that can easily be snapped between the fingers. Varieties include green and waxy yellow.

Cabbage: Well-trimmed, reasonably solid heads that are heavy for their size are the best quality. For green cabbage, the leaves should be medium green. Varieties include Savoy cabbage, with yellowish crimped leaves; Celery cabbage, often called Chinese cabbage; and red cabbage, identical to green cabbage except in color.

Carrots: Choose those that are firm, brightly-colored, smooth, clean, and well-shaped.

Cauliflower: Fresh cauliflower has bright green leaves surrounding the firm, closely-packed, creamy-white curd. Avoid heads that have yellowed or withered leaves attached. Leaves occasionally found growing through the curds do not affect quality.

Celery: Purchase celery having fresh branches brittle enough to snap easily. Avoid wilted looking stalks that feel rough or puffy. Pascal celery is the most common variety.

Cucumbers: Bright green cucumbers that are firm, well-shaped, and fresh-appearing are the best buy. Dull green ones are indicative of lower quality. Cucumbers are waxed before being sold to help retard evaporation and enhance the appearance.

Garlic: Consisting of many smaller sections, called cloves, garlic is usually purchased in bulbs. Pick those that are plump, firm, and have unbroken outer skins.

Mushrooms: Fresh mushrooms should look fresh and feel dry and firm. Small brown spots or opened caps indicate more mature mushrooms. These still have a delicate flavor.

Onions: Buy regular dry onions that are well-shaped, hard, and have dry skins. They should not be wet or feel soggy at the necks. Bermuda onions, perfect for salads or sandwiches, are flat and yellow or white. Green onions, sometimes called scallions, should have crisp green tops and white roots 2 to 3 inches long. Leeks look like large green onions and should also have bright green tops. Fresh chives are usually purchased as potted plants. Both roots and tops are used. Color should be bright green.

Parsley: Used mainly for garnish, parsley should be bright and fresh in appearance.

Peppers: The most common pepper is the green (bell) pepper. When fully mature, their color turns red. Choose those that have good shape, firm exterior, thick flesh, and bright, uniform glossy color.

Potatoes: "Baking" potatoes generally are too mealy in texture to be satisfactory for salads. The round, waxy types of potatoes are best for salads. They should have shallow eyes and be reasonably clean, smooth-skinned, and firm. Avoid those that are bruised, wilted, or sprouted. Some red potatoes are artificially colored with a non-toxic substance to help their appearance and preserve their freshness.

Radishes: Choose those that are smooth, crisp, firm, and well-formed. If the tops are still intact when purchased, they should be fresh and bright green.

Spinach: When buying spinach, look for fresh-appearing leaves with rich green color. Wilted or yellow leaves indicate spinach that is not fresh, therefore, undesirable.

Tomatoes: Handle these gently since ripe tomatoes are very delicate. Select those that are firm, well-formed, and free from blemishes. If not for immediate use, choose tomatoes having a greenish cast; ripen at room temperature. Avoid tomatoes that look yellow or wrinkled. The small cherry tomatoes are also good for salads. Their usual size is from 1 to 1½ inches but some are 2 inches in diameter.

SHOPPING FOR SALAD GREENS

Create tossed salads that boast flavor and appearance variety. Thanks to modern production and processing techniques, salad greens in assorted green shades and leaf shapes appear in grocery stores throughout the year. The salad green repertoire is not limited to the eight standards shown here. Leaf lettuce, for instance, comes in red-leafed or more ruffled salad-bowl versions.

Curly endive—narrow, fine, tight curls on heavy →
rib. Dark green outer curls; heart is pale.
   Selection: Crisp, fresh leaves; tender stalks.
   Storage: Keeps in plastic bag in crisper of refrigerator 1 week or more.
   Flavor: Slightly bitter.

Romaine—cylindrical or elongated head with coarse, stiff leaves. Has a heavy midrib.
   Selection: Well-trimmed, full head. Rich green outer leaves with minimum blemishes.
   Storage: Keeps in plastic bag in crisper of refrigerator about 1 week.
   Flavor: Sharp, butter-nut.

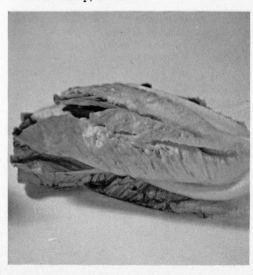

Escarole—rich green outer leaves; broad, slightly curly. Heart well-branched; appears bleached.
   Selection: Fresh, crisp, and tender.
   Storage: Keeps in plastic bag in crisper of refrigerator 1 week or more.
   Flavor: Slightly bitter.

Bibb lettuce—small cup-shaped head.
Selection: Soft-texture green leaves.
Storage: Keeps in plastic bag in crisper of re-frigerator a few days only.

Boston lettuce—soft head. Inner leaves feel oily.
Selection: Fairly firm head; fresh, soft-textured leaves. Big Boston leaves are brown on edges.
Storage: Keeps in plastic bag in crisper of re-frigerator 1 or 2 days.
Flavor: Sweet, delicate.

Leaf lettuce—loose, non-head forming leaves.
Selection: Soft, tender leaves. Avoid wilted or decayed-looking bunches.
Storage: Keeps in plastic bag in crisper of re-frigerator a few days only.
Flavor: Sweet, delicate (like Bibb).

Watercress—long stems; green round leaflets.
Selection: Bright green, crisp, and clean.
Storage: Put stems in jar of water; cover. Chill.
Flavor: Pungent, mustard-like.

Iceberg lettuce—most popular. Solid head.
Selection: Medium weight for size. Slight "give" when squeezed lightly. Leaves free from decay.
Storage: Keeps in plastic bag in crisper of re-frigerator about 1 week.
Flavor: Sweet, mild.

FOOD STORAGE GUIDE

Apples: To keep crisp and tangy, store in refrigerator or some equally cool spot.

Apricots and *Peaches:* Ripen at room temperature. Refrigerate to prevent spoilage.

Avocados: Ripen at room temperature; refrigerate (up to 3 days) till needed.

Berries: Refrigerate, unwashed and dry, immediately. Use quickly. Wash for use.

Citrus Fruits: Refrigerate to keep grapefruit, oranges, and all citrus fruits juicy.

Figs: Use immediately; refrigerate briefly.

Grapes: Refrigerate. Use quickly.

Kiwi: Need no refrigeration.

Mangoes: Ripen at room temperature. Use immediately or refrigerate briefly.

Melons: If kept at room temperature (1 to 3 days) before use, meat will ripen.

Nectarines: Refrigerate briefly.

Papayas: Ripen fruit at room temperature. Refrigerate fully-ripe fruit for brief period.

Pears: Ripen at room temperature. Refrigeration of ripe fruit prevents spoilage.

Persimmons: Ripen best at room temperature. Refrigerate ripe fruit for short time.

Plums: Refrigerate ripe fruit immediately.

Pomegranates: Store briefly at room temperature away from light. Refrigeration keeps fruit moist. May be kept frozen.

Vegetables may require one of the following storage methods—

Moist cold: Refrigerate, covered, in crisper bin, plastic bag, or covered jar.

Dry cold: Place in *cool*, dry, dark area.

Artichokes: Store briefly in moist cold.

Beans, Green and Wax: Store in moist cold.

Cabbages: Store in moist cold.

Carrots: Store in moist cold. Keep well.

Cauliflower: Store in moist cold.

Celery: Store in moist cold for crispness.

Cucumbers: Store in moist cold.

Garlic: Store, covered, in dry cold.

Onions: Store in dry, not necessarily cold area. Never store with potatoes. Absorb moisture from potatoes, causing decay.

Green Onions: Store briefly in moist cold.

Mushrooms: Store briefly in moist cold.

Parsley: Store briefly in moist cold.

Peppers: Store briefly in moist cold for crispness and flavor retention.

Potatoes: Store in dry cold as greening takes place rapidly at room temperatures. Affected potatoes have bitter taste.

Radishes: Store briefly in moist cold.

Spinach: Store briefly in moist cold to retain crispness and fresh flavor.

Tomatoes: Store briefly in moist cold.

 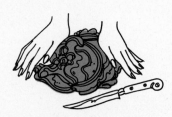 

To prepare lettuce for use, discard discolored or wilted leaves. Rinse thoroughly and quickly under cold water. For lettuce cups, core head, then run water through core to loosen. Drain; gently remove cups.

For lettuce cups from compact head—wash, core, and drain head. Turn top down on cutting board. Press with palms of hands, and gently push from side to side to loosen. Remove cups as needed.

Toss or drain greens for full-flavored salads. Toss leafy greens in clean kitchen towel or paper towels. Use rack or paper towels to drain thoroughly. Water dilutes dressing and dressing coats dry leaves evenly.

PREPARATION TIPS

Kitchen shears are faster and easier than a paring knife for seeding grapes. First, cut grapes in half, then snip out seeds. Grapes are ready to use.

Tomato skins loosen by plunging them for a few seconds in boiling water. Another method is to twirl them over a flame for just a moment.

Score raw potatoes around center. Cook, covered, in boiling salted water. Spear spuds with fork in score mark and start peeling there.

Cut avocados in half lengthwise; cup in palms of hands and gently twist. Tap seed with sharp edge of knife. Twist and lift or gently pry seed out.

To snip parsley, rinse thoroughly. Drain. Remove stems and put parsley in measuring cup. With shears in downward position, snip leaves.

When salad calls for marshmallows, use miniatures or snip large ones. Dip shears in confectioners' sugar or water first to prevent sticking.

To remove crown from whole pineapple, grasp crown in one hand and pineapple in other. Twist crown one way, pineapple the other.

To remove rind, cut wide strips from top to base, cutting just deep enough to remove eyes. Remove any remaining eyes with point of paring knife.

To serve pineapple in shell, quarter fruit and crown. Core. Using grapefruit knife, separate fruit from rind; slice and arrange in shell.

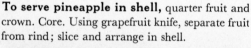

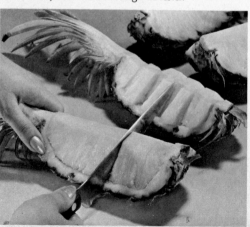

To section citrus fruit, peel fruit removing excess membrane. With knife, cut into center of fruit between one section and membrane. Slide knife down other side of section next to membrane.

To cook artichoke, remove stem, 1 inch of top, and leaf tips. Remove outer leaves. Brush cut edges with lemon juice. Simmer, covered, in boiling salted water and a little salad oil 20 to 30 minutes.

GELATIN TERMS TO KNOW

Almost firm: Chilled gelatin mixture appears set, but is sticky to the touch.

Firm: Chilled gelatin mixture is completely set and ready to unmold.

Fluffy, light and fluffy: Air is whipped into gelatin till volume is about double.

Foamy, light and foamy: Air is beaten into gelatin till mixture appears frothy.

Fold: Ingredients are added gently to mixture. With spatula, cut down through mixture; go across bottom then up and over, close to surface. Turn bowl often.

Gelatin, unflavored: One envelope of this granulated protein equals 1 tablespoon. This amount sets 2 cups liquid (including liquid used for softening).

Gelatin, flavored: This packaged mixture contains gelatin, sugar, fruit acids, flavors, and coloring. The 3-ounce size sets 2 cups liquid and 2 cups drained fruit.

Mounds when spooned: Chilled gelatin mounds when dropped from a spoon.

Partially set: Chilled gelatin is the consistency of unbeaten egg whites.

Soft peaks: Mixture is beaten till peaks form and tips curl when beaters are lifted.

Stiff peaks: Egg whites are beaten till peaks stand up straight when beaters are lifted, but whites are still moist and glossy.

GELATIN TECHNIQUES

Adding fruits, vegetables, meat, etc.: Chill dissolved gelatin till partially set; fold in food so that it will be evenly distributed throughout. If during chilling gelatin becomes too stiff, set bowl of gelatin in pan of hot water. Stir till gelatin is liquid again; rechill till partially set.

Adding carbonated beverages: Cool dissolved gelatin to room temperature. Rest carbonated beverage bottle on rim of bowl; pour slowly down side of bowl. Gently stir up and down. Chill immediately till firm.

Whipping souffle-type salads: Chill mixture of gelatin and mayonnaise or salad dressing till partially set, then whip till fluffy. Or, pour gelatin-mayonnaise mixture into freezer tray; chill in freezer till ice crystals form around edges. Whip till fluffy.

Unmolding gelatin salads: Loosen gelatin around edges of mold with spatula. Dip mold to rim in *warm* water for a *few seconds.* Tilt mold slightly easing gelatin away from one side to let air in. Tilt and rotate so air can loosen gelatin all the way around. Place serving platter upside down over mold. Hold platter and mold together; invert and shake gently to release. Carefully lift off mold. If gelatin does not release, tilt mold again or redip quickly in warm water.

Arranging fruit: Spoon thin layer of dissolved gelatin in bottom of mold. Arrange fruit. Chill till *almost* firm. Add remaining dissolved gelatin.

Preparing layered salads: Chill first gelatin layer till *almost* firm. Pour second layer over; chill till *almost* firm. Repeat layering as desired.

GARNISHING GLAMOUR

CUCUMBER BASKET

Hollow out a 3-inch length of unpared cucumber, leaving ¼-inch base and walls. Mark lengthwise strips around outside. Pare down every other strip of peel, *almost* to base. Crisp in ice water; drain. Pare strips of peel from remaining cucumber. Shape in circles; secure with wooden picks at base of basket. Fill with mayonnaise. Trim with parsley.

ORANGE CHRYSANTHEMUM

Score peel of 2 or more oranges into 8 sections, *cutting to, but not through,* base of peel. Gently remove peel from fruit, keeping shell in one piece. Pull fruit sections of 1 orange apart slightly; remove excess membrane. Use remaining fruit for salad.

With scissors, cut sectioned peels into small "petals," *cutting to, but not through,* bases. Replace prepared orange in 1 shell. Insert this shell into remaining petaled shells.

VEGETABLE FLOWERS

Slice pared large carrot and turnip crosswise, ⅛ inch thick. Cut flowers using cookie and tiny hors d'oeuvres cutters.

To prepare centerpiece pictured, thread green onion tops over wooden skewers. Attach desired flowers to ends of skewers. Use green onion and carrot pieces for centers.

CITRUS GARNISHES

Rose: Starting at stem end of lemon and/or lime, cut peel around fruit in continuous spiral. With stem end in center, curl into rose shape. Secure with wooden pick. For larger rose, curl several peels together.

Cartwheels: Slice fruit ⅛ inch thick. Notch peel around outside as desired.

Twists: Make 1 cut into fruit slice; twist.

Curls: Cut ⅛-inch citrus slice in half, *cutting to, but not through,* one edge of peel. Remove fruit from one half. Curl peel.

Tomato Roses: Turn tomato, stem end down. With sharp knife, cut 5 or 6 petals, cutting through skin but not into seed pocket. Gently separate petals slightly. Season with salt and pepper to taste. For added color, sprinkle center with sieved hard-cooked egg yolks. Use to garnish buffet platters or tossed salads. Tiny cherry tomato rosettes are particularly suitable to garnish individual salad servings.

Turnip Lilies: Here's an elegant-looking trim that's simple to make. For each lily, cut 2 *thin* crosswise pared turnip slices. Curve one slice into cone shape. Shape second slice around cone in opposite direction. Insert thin strip of carrot down center of cone. Secure lily with wooden picks. Crisp in ice water. Rutabaga slices are a good substitute if turnip is not available.

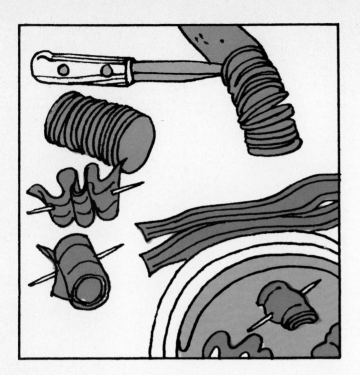

Carrot Corkscrews: Insert point of short-bladed paring knife into pared whole carrot, *cutting to, but not through,* center at slight angle; rotate carrot slowly, cutting a continuous spiral. Make deeper cut into carrot, if necessary, to make corkscrew flexible. Chill in ice water to open.

Carrot Curls: Rest pared carrot on cutting surface. Shave a thin and wide lengthwise strip of carrot with parer, pushing parer away from you. Roll up long slice; secure with wooden pick. Crisp in ice water; remove pick before serving.

Carrot Zigzags: Rest pared whole carrot on cutting surface. Make a thin, wide lengthwise strip of carrot with parer, cutting away from you. Thread on wooden pick accordion style. Crisp in ice water; remove pick before serving.

Fruit Baskets: Halve large grapefruit. With grapefruit or paring knife, cut around each section to loosen fruit; remove fruit from sections, leaving membrane intact. Snip out whole membrane.

Leaving 1 inch uncut in center of opposite sides, cut around each grapefruit half with paring knife ⅜ inch below rim to make basket handles. Carefully lift up the 2 resulting cut strips and tie together with ribbon of desired color.

Refill cavity of basket with a fruit salad combination containing the grapefruit sections. If desired, top fruit with miniature scoops of sherbet made with spoon or melon ball cutter. Serve immediately.

For smaller fruit salad serving, make basket from large orange, following directions above. Use orange sections in the fruit salad.

Radish Roses: Cut root tip off radish, then cut 4 or 5 thin petals around radish, leaving a little red between the petals. Use a grapefruit knife or point of paring knife. (If desired, leave on some green leaves at stem for trim.) Chill in ice water till petals spread open like a flower. Use radish roses as a relish or plate trim.

Petaled Daisies: Starting at root tip, score 6 petals on radish with point of knife. Following markings and beginning at tip, cut thin petals following shape of radish *almost* to base (stem end). Chill in ice water till petals open. Use as a relish or plate trim.

Radish Accordions: Cut long radishes crosswise, *cutting to, but not through*, in 8 narrow slices. Chill in ice water so slices will fan out, accordion style.

Scored Cucumbers: For fancy cucumber slices, run tines of fork lengthwise down unpared cucumber, pressing to break through peel. Repeat around entire cucumber. Slice straight across or on the bias. Use in tossed salads or as a relish.

Pickle Fans: Slice pickle lengthwise *almost* to stem end, making thin slices. Spread each fan and press uncut end of pickle so fan will hold its shape.

Stuffed Pickle Slices: Cut thin slice from stem end of large dill pickle. Hollow pickle with apple corer. Stuff with softened cream cheese or any spreading cheese. Chill well, then slice crosswise.

Pickle Accordions: (not shown) Cut off ends of pickles, then slice crosswise, *cutting to, but not through*, pickle. Bend pickle gently so slices separate at top.

Zigzag Melon Bowls: For attractive serving "bowls," cut small cantaloupe in half zigzag fashion by inserting knife into center of melon at an angle. Pull knife out and make next cut at reverse angle. Repeat around melon. Pull two halves apart; remove seeds. It might be easier to make heavy paper pattern and draw where cuts are to be made; carve along lines. Fill bowls with a salad mixture.

Scalloped Melon Bowl: Set watermelon on end. Cut thin slice off bottom to make it sit flat. Cut top third off melon. Using a cup as guide, trace scallops around edge of melon. Carve scalloped edge following pattern. Scoop out fruit. Using melon ball cutter, if desired, or large spoon, cut up pieces of fruit to be used in salad. Refill shell with fruit mixture.

Apple Rings: Pare or leave peel on apples. Cut out core using apple corer. Slice to desired thickness. Keep bright by brushing with ascorbic acid color keeper or lemon juice mixed with water.

Frosted Grapes: Combine slightly beaten egg white and a little water. Brush mixture over cluster of grapes using pastry brush. Sprinkle with granulated sugar; dry on rack. Use as a plate garnish.

Cheese Apples: Moisten shredded cheese with mayonnaise or salad dressing. Roll in balls. Make an indentation in each end. Insert whole clove in one end and half a green wooden pick in other end. Roll in paprika for rosy color.

Make balls from process cheese by cutting with melon ball cutter or forming with hands. Repeat with cloves, picks, and paprika.

INDEX

A-B